WHOSE SPECIAL NEED?

WHOSE SPECIAL NEED?

Some Perceptions of
Special Educational Needs

SARAH SANDOW
(editor)

P·C·P
Paul Chapman
Publishing Ltd

Editorial material, selection, chapter 1, chapter 7, chapter 11 and 12, 1994 © Sarah
Sandow. All other material copyright Paul Chapman Publishing.

Paul Chapman Publishing Ltd
144 Liverpool Road
London
N1 1LA

British Library Cataloguing in Publication Data

Whose Special Need?
 I. Sandow, Sarah
 371.9

 ISBN 1 85396 219 8

Typeset by Hewer Text Composition Services, Edinburgh
Printed and bound by Athenaeum Press Ltd., Newcastle-upon-Tyne

A B C D E F G H 9 8 7 6 5 4

Contents

Preface

This book is intended for teachers and student teachers. Some will already have knowledge of special educational needs, professionally or personally, others will see it as a new and perhaps alarming responsibility. Special educational need is a multifaceted concept, and the view of each individual is rooted in the philosophy and tradition of different specialisms, modified and structured by personal experience.

The approaches considered here are by no means exhaustive, but they provide an insight into a number of points of view, and an opportunity for reflection, in which account can be taken of a range of perspectives, as the reader constructs her own.

It will be noted that I have written 'her' in the previous sentence. The English language does not allow us to be gender independent, and as teaching children with special educational needs is primarily (though not exclusively) a female specialism, I have reversed the usual convention, in order to avoid the irritation of 'his/her' and the ungrammatical 'their'.

Throughout the book, at the end of each chapter, the reader will find a number of suggestions, questions she should ask herself, further reading, exercises and tasks which may be illuminating. Some of these are derived from tasks set on in-service courses, which have helped teachers to reflect profitably on their own experience.

I would like to thank my collaborators for their contributions, and for their speed of response at a time of considerable overload. I am especially indebted to my colleague Philip Garner for his valuable comments on the first drafts of my own contributions. Thanks also to Lynn Young and Ruth Corben for allowing me to quote from their course assignments. I am grateful for permission to include a short section from Raymond Briggs' *The Man*, a fable which illuminates the emotions, the frustrations and the dilemmas of the helpers and the helped.

Finally, I express my very great thanks to Jamie Davidson for his indispensable help and patience in preparing the final document.

Sarah Sandow

The Contributors

David Anderson-Ford is a principal lecturer in the Department of Health and Paramedical Studies at the West London Institute (College of Brunel University). He is the author of a number of works on the legal system as applied to mental health and special education, including *The Social Worker's Law Book* (second edition 1992, Butterworths).

Carol Aubrey was a primary school teacher before training as an educational psychologist in the early 1980s. She joined University College, Cardiff, as a lecturer in education before taking up her present post as senior lecturer in education at the University of Durham, where she is course leader for the PGCE (Primary) course. She has written extensively on educational psychology and her current research interests include looking critically at pedagogy for special needs and the exploration of teachers' pedagogical subject knowledge in early-years maths teaching.

Jenny Corbett is senior lecturer in education at the University of East London. She is a member of the editorial board of the *British Educational Research Journal* and of *Disability and Society*. She is currently researching into post-school provision for students with disabilities and learning difficulties.

Philip Garner is senior lecturer in the Department of Education at the West London Institute, where he is course leader for the diploma and master's courses in special educational needs, and also teaches on initial teacher training courses. He has published extensively on comparative special education, with special reference to eastern Europe, and his current research interests include self-advocacy for students with special needs and provision for students with emotional and behavioural difficulties.

Viv Hinchcliffe was a teacher of children with severe learning difficulties before joining the staff of the Department of Education at the West London Institute, where he leads diploma and master's courses in severe learning difficulties. His main research interest is in developing social cognition in children with severe learning difficulties.

Sarah Sandow is reader in education at the West London Institute, where she co-ordinates master's degrees. She has researched a range of issues relating to parent-professional relations in the context of special education, and is interested in all aspects of interprofessional collaboration.

Anne Stokes was formerly a deputy headteacher in a comprehensive school. She is now a trained counsellor and a lecturer at Bristol University and at the West London Institute, where she leads courses on counselling. She also has a private counselling practice.

Jannet Wright is a speech therapist who is a senior lecturer at the London Hospital's College of Speech Sciences. She is currently researching the role of the speech therapist and interprofessional relations.

Frontispiece

So . . . You're not a fairy, you're not an ET, you're not a gnome. So what are you?

I'm me! Just shut up! It's insulting to be asked what I am the whole time. It implies I'm not human.

Well, you're not normal, are you?

Depends what you mean by normal.

You're not like us, are you?

Who is us? Your little family?

Well, yes . . . if you like . . .

So are you the normal by which everyone is to be judged?

Well . . . um . . . I don't know really . . . I'll get you another biscuit, shall I?

1

More Ways than One: Models of Special Needs

Sarah Sandow

What do we mean by the term 'special educational needs'? Each of us brings with us the baggage of a lifetime in which we have absorbed a view of the subject gleaned from our childhood experience, our reading and observations derived from other media, all of which have become part of a construct of special education without any conscious effort on our part.

If we attempt to unravel this experience we find a number of contributing factors, which may be described as 'models', or sets of beliefs and understandings which have originated at different eras and which have left a trail behind which informs our perceptions today.

The magical model
The magical model is pre-scientific. It originated before the era of the Enlightenment in the late eighteenth century, at a time when disabilities were perceived as the result of acts of God, or conversely of the Devil, and were treated as miraculous events beyond the control of the individual parent.

Here began the idea of the 'changeling' visited upon the family by some evil spirit, whose actions may be triggered by some apparently harmless event. Perhaps the story of Sleeping Beauty epitomizes this approach. Witches, including those in fairy tales, were always ugly, deformed, possessed the evil eye, and were accompanied by terrifying 'familiars'. So, people with harelips, club feet, squints or other deformities were regarded with fear. Left-handedness was similarly suspect, or 'sinister'. Such views received official sanction: the publication in the late fifteenth century of the *Malleus Maleficarum*, the *Hammer of Witches*, was approved by Pope Innocent VIII.

Today, in some societies, the outstretched palm or the handprint represents the protection from the evil eye directed by the stranger. A different kind of visitation is recalled in the word *cretin* for one, now mercifully rare, condition, which derives from *cretien* (or *Christian*), meaning holy.

The ideas of sin and the phenomenon of illness were very confused. Before the Reformation there were relatively few days in the calendar when sexual intercourse was permitted, therefore a disabled child could be seen as the result of 'excess' on the wrong day.

This model obviously survives where people are superstitious, but also where a very unsophisticated view of causation is taken, or where people are fatalistic about the events of life. What is not understood must be magic.

The implication of such a view is that education for the affected child is impossible and may be almost sacrilegious: 'flying in the face of nature'. The need to accept 'God's will' or reject the Devil's work takes precedence over any attempt at remediation.

There was also a fascination about such people, whether seen in freak shows, like John Merrick, the 'elephant man', or marvelled at, like Caspar Hauser, the *idiot savant*. Such individuals, by their difference, confirm our normality. Caliban, Barnaby Rudge, the Wild Boy of Aveyron, and modern autists may be reassuring as well as alarming. Several ruling families such as the Spanish Hapsburgs and the Empress Maria Theresa of Russia surrounded themselves with such people. 'Lord, I thank thee that I am not as other men are' may be thought, if not said, in this context as well as that of the Pharisee and the Publican. That which we do not understand we ascribe to the supernatural.[1]

The moral model

The moral model suggests that mankind is perfectible, and that it is by and large his own responsibility to become as perfect as possible. What 'perfect' means will change from time to time, but underlying the concept is the theory that human beings are creatures of intent.

> What men are and what they may become is very much a function of how they treat themselves and one another; in this sense, if in no other, beings in a moral world may have quite a different quality to them than entities in a physical world with a fixed nature.
>
> (Shotter, 1980, p. 19)

Morality, in this view of mankind extends to the teacher and the taught. Each has responsibilities. John Woolman, the Quaker, expressed this in religious terms in 1758: 'to watch the spirit of children, to nurture them in gospel love and labour to help them against that which would mar the beauty of their minds, is a debt we owe them', and the Quaker keepers of the York Retreat treated the insane with a respect and gentleness incongruent with their time (see

Chapter 7). The philosophers of the Enlightenment, accepting the view that 'there is nothing in the mind that was not first in the senses', set out, like Itard (Lane, 1976), to train the senses in order to educate the mind. However, the taught, too, are perceived as intentional individuals; therefore they are, or will become, responsible for their own learning. A rather less sympathetic version of this approach applied to learning difficulty leads to the belief that failure to learn is finally the child's own fault, and disability is equated with idleness or with wilful refusal to learn. So, when this view is paramount, we hear phrases like 'bone idle', 'he just won't learn', 'could do better', and the dunce is (or was) put in the corner. Victorian philanthropy, adapting its own version of the moral model, required a grateful recipient, and reflected the view that children need to be tamed, made civilized, and valued according to the degree that they accept this civilization. So we define the social by the antisocial, the civilized by the uncivilized, the hard-working by the lazy. It is a small step from this to the Poor Law view of the 'undeserving poor' who were seen as responsible for their own poverty, by fecklessness, alcohol and improvidence. Confidence, enthusiasm and hope (see page 91) were replaced by guilt, apathy and despair.

The medical model
The medical model is the most commonly cited explanation of special educational needs. The doctor in the nineteenth century was himself subject to ideas about causality which, derived from those examined above, was never perceived as social but always hereditary. Impotent in the face of most conditions, he sought only to prevent disability, and attempted to do so by warning the population of what were perceived to be dangerous causative behaviours. It goes without saying that poverty, malnutrition or Godfrey's Cordial (opium administered to soothe the crying babies of working women) were not regarded as significant.

Three individuals combined to promote a very negative image of the causation of disability. John Langdon Down (1866) proposed his 'ethnic classification of idiocy', which included not only those with the syndrome which now bears his name (whom he called 'Mongolian idiots')' but also those with a number of other conditions each of which he identified as a throwback to a less effective form of *Homo sapiens*, all of course compared unfavourably to the white Caucasian type.

A French physician, Morel, proposed a 'Theory of Degeneracy' in which he sought to explain the correlation between poverty and disability by suggesting an actual and sequential series of generational links between alcoholism and 'social corruption' through congenital weakness and a nervous disposition, to psychosis and, eventually, idiocy (Morel, 1857).

Thirdly, Darwin's *Origin of Species* (1860) promoted the idea of the survival of the fittest as a continuous process of natural selection. At this time there was no real understanding of the mechanism of heredity, the transmitting fluid was presumed to be blood, and certain diseases such as tuberculosis and syphilis, or behaviours such as prostitution were perceived as 'poisoners of the germ plasm'. In fact, tuberculosis was seen (as in *La Dame aux Camellias* or *East Lynne*) as being directly caused by promiscuity, rather than correlated with it. We recall such ideas in expressions like 'bad blood', 'blood will out' and 'blood's thicker than water'.

Functioning in such a climate it is not surprising that doctors, unable in any case to offer more than morphine and sympathy, were greatly influenced by the 'scientific' nature of such theories and sought to practise preventive medicine in advocating continence, and theorized about causation in terms of the identi-fication of precipitating factors in previous generations. The 'within child' aspect of the medical model thus became a 'within family' matter. It would be hardly surprising if the afflicted family felt themselves even more separated from the doctor than by mere social class, and even less surprising that there are so many stories (such as *Jane Eyre*) which include the mad woman or man in the attic, unacknowledged and untreated.

The doctor is first a diagnostician: diagnosis is supposed to lead to cure. 'If only we knew the cause . . .' people say as they seek, perhaps in memory of those times, reassurance that it was not their fault. The doctor is still the representative of our betters; people tidy up for him remembering a structured society in which each knew his place: the rich man in his castle and the poor man at his gate. The present day doctors' dilemmas, described by Corbett in Chapter 4, are different from the fears and prejudices of former times, but some effects of these are still extant, including the strong belief in the doctor as omnipotent, the social class gap between doctor and patient, the assumption of heredity as the basis for handicap, and the demand for cure via diagnosis. Such concentration on factors within the child meant that, firstly, no attention was paid to external contexual factors (such as recognizing that tuberculosis was a concomitant of prostitution, not the result of it), and, secondly, a concentration on difference and disability. Potts (1983) describes the so-called objective methods of diagnosis practised by physicians such as Tredgold usually involving *post hoc* identifications of 'aments' based on appalling simplifica-tions, and draws an alarming parallel with modern practice in the 1980s.

The intellectual model
The medical model with its emphasis on constitutional or innate characteristics leads naturally to a view of special educational needs which is rooted in

eugenics both in terms of ability and personality. Simply, the argument was that as individuals' birth inheritance was all powerful, there could be no significant change in intellectual performance over time. It must be remembered that before 1870, although elementary education was offered to some working-class children in church schools, this did not extend much beyond the three Rs and religious instruction. The revised code stipulated what was to be assessed, and the children's success determined the remuneration of teachers. What we would now call secondary education only existed for the upper classes, and even then it focused on mathematics, Greek and Latin. (Science was seen as a rather unsuitable activity for the ruling class.) Intellectual skill was actually not as useful to ordinary people as social or craft skills, and intelligence as a concept was hardly recognized independently of social class. The rich, by definition, were capable of, and needed, a classical education. The poor, by definition, did not. In fact it was perceived by the ruling class as highly dangerous to educate them at all. The idea that any of the poor were equal in intellectual terms to their betters was dangerous radicalism, and could lead to revolution, of which the upper classes had been afraid since 1789: 'There is still . . . a lurking, though unexpressed fear, that the lower orders may be too highly educated, and there is a sentiment, the offspring of that fear, that the State has done its duty when it imparts the rudiments of knowledge' (Playfair, 1870). Those rudiments were identified as, for example, the ability to give correct arithmetical answers or to read aloud with accuracy, but not necessarily, in either case, to do so with understanding (Selleck, 1968).

Consequently the idea of any identification of individuals by intellectual criteria was simply irrelevant. This view was challenged towards the end of the century as the mental testing movement developed, though some of the early attempts at measuring intelligence show how difficult it was to get a purchase on the nature of intellectual skill. Cattell's (1890) list shows great dependence on the psychophysiological preoccupations of nineteenth century psychology (Miller, 1973).

(1) *Dynamometer pressure.* How tightly can the hand squeeze?
(2) *Rate of movement.* How quickly can the hand be moved through a distance of 50 cm?
(3) *Sensation areas.* How far apart must two points be on the skin to be recognized as two rather than one?
(4) *Pressure causing pain.* How much pressure on the forehead is necessary to cause pain?
(5) *Least noticeable difference in weight.* How large must the difference be between two weights before it is reliably detected?
(6) *Reaction time for sound.* How quickly can the hand be moved at the onset of an auditory signal?

   (7) *Time for naming colours.* How long does it take to name a strip of
        ten different coloured papers?
   (8) *Bisection of a 50 cm line.* How accurately can one point to the centre
        of an ebony rule?
   (9) *Judgement of 10 sec. time.* How accurately can an interval of 10
        seconds be judged?
  (10) *Number of letters remembered on once hearing.* How many letters,
        ordered at random, can be repeated exactly after one hearing?

Later, when Binet's tests crossed the Channel there was a gradual acknowledgement that intellectual skill did breach the class barrier. However, the logic
adduced by Cyril Burt to justify some of his early testing experiments
(Hearnshaw, 1979) is evidence that this was still a difficult concept for the
ruling class to accept.

   Burt was in fact the main influence behind the tripartite education system
which set in stone for many years the idea of inborn differentiated intellectual
characteristics, which could be identified before the age of eleven and which
would remain substantially unchanged ever after, 'even into extreme old age'
(Spearman, 1904). The idea took root that verbal reasoning skills and spatial
mechanical skills occurred in different groups which required different forms of
education. A third group, in which neither group of skills was regarded as
particularly apparent, formed the remaining element in the system. The fact
that social classes were unequally represented in the three groups surprised and
concerned nobody. The idea of the permanence of IQ, once established, was all
pervading.

   The Education Act 1944 identified ten categories of handicap and continued
the tradition of dividing children on a more or less permanent basis into groups
with different perceived skills and destined for different social classes. In the
1960s, following the recognition by psychologists in the UK and the USA that
'intelligence' as defined by intelligence tests was by no means fixed, a new
process of social engineering was undertaken, in which, by the establishment of
educational priority areas and the initiation of the comprehensive school
system, it was hoped to make a wider range of options available to children
who had previously been restricted to a very few.

   However, the intellectual model is very persistent. Currently, the National
Curriculum assessment system is one example of the *de facto* acceptance of
such divisions. For example, the system does not permit pupils to score above
the level permitted in the group to which they have been assigned by the
teacher. Thus the intellectual model is now reinforced by statute. If we carry
this particular piece of conceptual baggage with us, it is likely to inform the
way we respond to individual children, and to affect the way we differentiate

the curriculum in ordinary or in special schools. Hence the establishment of the 'developmental' curriculum in schools for children with severe learning difficulties into areas (social, cognitive, motor, communication, creative) which are essentially anti-intellectual, and the ideas about 'disapplying' parts of the National Curriculum for children with moderate learning difficulties, which usually means the exclusion of modern foreign languages.[2]

The very use of the term 'learning difficulties' which has been adopted in the Education Act 1981 suggests that special educational needs are finally to be identified in intellectual terms. In Chapter 3 Aubrey outlines the dilemma for the educational psychologist in the 1990s who now feels that her role is being externally redefined, and not for the better.

The social competence model

An alternative to the intellectual model is social competence. Individuals are accepted on the basis of the degree to which they conform behaviourally to the norms of the time. In the late nineteenth and early twentieth centuries, the influence of the eugenics movement made behaviour as well as intelligence a factor in inheritance. The establishment of industrial schools where girls and boys 'rescued' from the streets were taught domestic and trade skills (separately, of course) was followed by the segregation of those who might contaminate the normal population into 'colonies', asylums usually situated in the countryside, away from the opportunities and temptations of cities and towns. The Mental Deficiency Act 1913 included a new category, the 'moral defective' (as evidenced from sexual 'immorality'), and these too, mainly young women with illegitimate babies, were incarcerated to protect society. The early twentieth century fear of contamination was very powerful, and the disgust at illegitimate parenthood extended of course to the children themselves. It is notable in this context that adoption was not made legal until 1927. Social competence, however, unlike the intellectual model, is a very utilitarian one. The very incompetent were segregated to protect society and the curriculum in special schools was designed to make the pupils employable, albeit in menial tasks. Much later, Gunzburg (1966) based his 'Progress Assessment Chart' on the premise that intellectual measurement alone was an inadequate and unhelpful way of assessing people with mental handicaps. The chart was one of the first assessment systems which had clear curricular implications. It was also one of the few where assessment was independent of chronological age, thus freeing the individual from the tyranny of norm-referenced assessment. Wilson and Cowell (1983) have proposed the abandonment of the intellectual model altogether in favour of a version of social competence which has echoes of spirituality. However, the injunction to 'be good, sweet

maid, and let who will be clever' has never been fully honoured, even by those
urging it.

Disadvantage

It was not until the Second World War, when large numbers of inner-city
children were evacuated to the country, that the deprivation experienced by
many children was made apparent. For the first time there was a developing
understanding that the causes of disability could be traced to these conditions
which were imposed on, not caused by, their victims. The National Child
Development Study (Essen and Wedge, 1982a) produced mounting evidence
that poor educational achievement was correlated with a number of disadvantaging factors, notably poor housing, large or single-parent families and
low income. While this may seem obvious in the 1990s, the prevailing
disposition to look only within the child and his family for the causes of
special educational needs in children meant that these findings were both
unexpected and alarming. In the post-war welfare state there was a new
impetus to seek ways to compensate for the circumstances in which children
were living. Physically, children were weighed and measured and provided with
milk, orange juice and vitamin supplements. In the 1960s the influence of the
Headstart programmes was felt from the USA. Educational Priority Areas were
identified in which nursery education and extra funding for schools were
provided. A massive housing boom sought to replace the pre-war slums and to
house the many displaced by war. The eleven-plus examination was phased out
and the comprehensive system, built upon the idea that schools should cater for
an infinite variety of learning styles and speeds, was initiated. The idea of
education as compensation was born.

   However, whereas at the start the idea was that education could compensate
for society's disadvantaging structures, an alternative view began to prevail,
that education was compensating for the inadequacies of individual homes.
The attempts to train parents in some of the Headstart and other early
intervention programmes suggested as much. Although Bernstein's (1961)
system of restricted and elaborated linguistic codes was not intended to be
pejorative, it was certainly perceived by teachers and academics that the home
environment of many children was linguistically impoverished. The Bullock
Report (1975) with its injunction to 'bathe children in language' certainly made
this assumption. Although socio-linguists such as Labov (1969) questioned the
received view that working-class children were disadvantaged by their families,
and proposed that non-standard English had a structural validity and strength
of its own, many schools continued to see themselves as making up for the
inadequacies of home life. The findings of Tizard *et al.* (1980) about the quality

and complexity of parents' interactions with their children were a source of astonishment to many.[3] Thus, the idea of disadvantage as an explanatory model of disability, while seductive, is in fact more complex and perhaps less humanitarian than was at first thought.

The social conspiracy model

It has been suggested above that the normal is defined by the abnormal. The very existence of norms for behaviour or performance creates the need for some individuals to be outside those norms; but the norms themselves are variable, and depend on the 'needs' of society at any time. Tomlinson (1982) regarded the expansion of special education in recent years with deep suspicion, stating that the new 'special-needs industry' had the effect of marginalizing more and more children with a greater variety of identified handicaps, while providing employment for an increasing number of professionals. The Warnock figure of 'one in five' children with special needs at some point in their educational life (Croll and Moses, 1985) can be said to label, at least temporarily, a significant proportion of children in school as abnormal.

The situation arises because of the psychometric system of measuring human characteristics which is expressed as a continuum between two extremes with normality occupying more or less of the middle ground. The normal section of the continuum varies with the characteristic and its significance for society. Thus a wide range of mathematical skills is included within the normal part of the scale, and at each end 'can't add up' and 'senior wrangler' are both seen as abnormal (even though the former is regarded with derision and the latter with awe). A continuum for 'honesty' might be a slightly different shape, but the principle still applies. Administratively, we have provided for the mathematical dunce and the senior wrangler by providing cut-off points, such as examinations, and have provided education for each by reference to the size of the population in each section. Thus if only 2 per cent of the school population (those who are usually the subjects of statements of special educational needs) are identified as abnormal, this presents a different philosophical, organizational and financial situation from that in which 20 per cent are identified as having special needs. Tomlinson's view is that in extending the range of special provision for nominally altruistic reasons, an increasing percentage of pupils are identified as abnormal, with disastrous results for them. The increased number of professionals engaged in teaching, testing, managing, examining and supporting them has then an interest in preserving the 'special-needs industry' irrespective of the needs of the pupils. Indeed, this book (and Tomlinson's) are part of this industry.

It is not comfortable to question one's own altruism. Many of those reading this book will have come to be involved in special education for humanitarian reasons, but it is salutary at least to consider how dependent we become on the existence of children with special educational needs. It is also important to recognize that it is only by identifying those beyond the pale that we are able to decide who should be included within it. Classifying and ordering people, experiences, skills, facilities and so on is so much part of our lives that we find it hard to manage without it. The 1981 Act swept away the distinctions between categories of disability, in favour of the simple definition of 'special educational needs'. In practice new categories have replaced the old: 'severe learning difficulties' (SLD) instead of severely educationally subnormal (ESN(S)), 'moderate learning difficulties' (MLD) instead of ESN(M), 'emotional and behavioural difficulties' (EBD) instead of maladjusted, and so on.

Conclusion

This list has not exhausted all the possible models of special needs. Perhaps there may be others, but these represent the most common explanatory systems. Put simply, we can see disability as the result of supernatural, natural, or systematic agency. Probably each of us uses an amalgamation of all three. The following extract is the result of one teacher's self-examination on the topic.

> I do not find it a pleasurable experience examining my childhood memories of special needs. For a start the term 'special need' was unheard of; people with whatever disability were commonly known by some crass term relating to their disability.
>
> One of my earlier experiences was bringing my mother's wrath to bear when referring to a boy with asthma (and resultant pallor) as 'Ghostie', especially when she discovered we actually called him that as a taunt. The attitude fostered in me was obviously one of 'humanity' as in being humane. My colleague also remembers her cousin having a baby with Down's syndrome, being told it was 'for the best' when the infant died. I used to see a girl with Down's syndrome while waiting to go to Guides; she was older and a Ranger. I never made an effort to interact with her, although she was obviously independent enough to travel to the church hall on her own (which might now suggest to me the level of her ability), feeling incapable of doing so, a little embarrassed, a little overawed. A lady lived in our neighbourhood who was 'mentally retarded.' She looked somewhat unusual, wearing ribbons and bows in her greying hair. I remember being a little frightened of her.
>
> I am deliberately understating these attitudes because up to my teens I don't recall any strong emotions. However, from my teens comes my most powerful memory. I was watching a young woman with cerebral

palsy being interviewed on television after gaining a university degree. Her speech was extremely slurred and her face contorted as she spoke. I was alone and I couldn't stop laughing. I felt excruciatingly guilty, so much so I was trying to stop myself laughing. There were no pressures from anyone else, just my own internalized attitudes.

It is difficult to pick out a prominent 'model' of special needs experienced in my formative years. Certainly the 'magic' model is in there somewhere, the awe and the fear. But also a 'benevolent' model which I now know to be so handicapping to the person with a disability. It was never suggested to me that I should make positive efforts to relate to people with disabilities but I was left in no doubt it was wrong to ridicule them. My colleague was brought up with a different attitude, that people with disabilities were to be treated like anyone else and were part of normal life – a 'normalizing' model. I have subsequently found that a number of my colleagues received this message and wonder if it holds any correlation with entering this kind of work.

(Lynn Young, a teacher of children with SLD)

Notes

(1) I am indebted to Bryan Seagrove, archivist of the British and Foreign Schools Society, for advice on this section.

(2) I do not mean here to criticize the 'developmental curriculum', merely to identify its origin.

(3) It is interesting to note that none of these arguments appears to have been considered in 1993 as the National Curriculum Council prepares to impose 'standard English' on five-year-olds.

For the reader

What is your earliest memory of people with special educational needs or disabilities? With which 'model' of special needs did you grow up? Like the teacher quoted above, think this out for yourself and explore it with a colleague.

Introduction to Chapters 2 and 3

The next two chapters represent two aspects of the legal framework, its origins and effects. David Anderson-Ford first outlines the general system by which laws are created and identifies how this process applies to special education. The statutory provisions of the 1981 Act in particular were an attempt to clothe a principle – equal opportunity – in language which would be enabling but would not lead to too much expenditure. It is notable in this respect that the regulations for making statements of special educational need were not issued until 1983, suggesting that the legislators already knew they had a tiger by the tail. The cases cited by Anderson-Ford are all related to more or less successful attempts to secure judicial review of local education authority (LEA) decisions about provision, mainly *where* that provision should be made. The actual nature of that provision and the degree to which it should deviate in kind from that provided in ordinary schools was never, in the legal context, fully discussed.

Carol Aubrey devotes the first few pages of her chapter to a consideration of the implications of the legislation from the point of view of the educational psychologist. She makes it clear that the imprecision of the underlying concepts, never fully stated in the tautological definition of special need and provision in the Education Act 1981, has tended to obfuscate rather than to clarify a new way of thinking. She asks whether the goal of social integration in adult life is best served by educational integration. Arising out of this, Aubrey considers concomitant changes in the psychologist's role and questions whether the extended support which educational psychologists (who are all, of course, trained teachers) have provided in schools, can survive in the 1990s.

Educational psychology has tried to shed its preoccupation with intellectual deficit and psychometry in the past twenty years, but perhaps, as Aubrey suggests, it may have to return there in future.

Reading these two chapters, it is salutary to recognize that while within a legal framework, lawyers continue to try to make the legislation 'work', educational psychologists are already finding it at best constricting and, at worst, counterproductive.

2

Legal Aid: How Special Education is Defined in Law

David Anderson-Ford

The legal context

Before giving detailed consideration to the law as it relates to children with special needs, it may perhaps be prudent to consider some fundamental issues by way of background. Rules, regulations and occasionally, somewhat para-doxically, a lack of them, appear to fill our daily lives. Additionally, the citizen (in the matter under discussion often the parent or guardian) is seemingly faced with a secret and impenetrable world of jargon, and unfamiliar, confusing and often conflicting interpretations attributed to the written word.

Often, policies implemented from the best of intentions can become a game of words, played in turn (in the case of special educational needs) by the providers of services, such as local educational authorities, by local appeals committees and by the courts. Attempting to understand the 'letter of the law' can frequently become a self-defeating exercise.

In the light of this, it becomes important to understand the contextualization of issues within a legal framework. For example, what is the function of law and what is it for? A simple definition may usefully provide a starting point:

A system of rules, enforced by the State, which regulates, human activity within a defined geographical area.

Legal rules differ from, say, scientific rules in that they give guidance upon the consequences of particular types of behaviour, and this guidance is enforced by the state. Scientific rules, on the other hand, give no guidance. They are purely statements of fact and, in any event, are not concerned in particular with human behaviour.

It is, however, more difficult to draw a distinction between legal rules and moral rules. As we shall see, the Warnock Committee, (DES, 1978), concluded that 'education was a track along which every child and adult had a right to walk, a right of way'. This may be considered to be a statement of moral principle, but an important distinction lies in the fact that law originates from outside the individual, whereas an individual is free to set his or her own moral standards and to depart from those standards.

It must be said that general statements of moral principle often become embedded in the law by consensus, as the Education Act 1981 subsequently demonstrated, but the liaison is not always without difficulty (take the issue of abortion, for example). One particular characteristic of legal rules which is inextricably bound up with morality is the view that there is a moral obligation to obey the law – 'Without public confidence no system of justice can succeed' (Lord Hailsham) – and law provides the essential framework within which society functions by attempting to:

- maintain social order;
- recognize and define legal relationships between individuals;
- provide a means of resolving disputes between individuals;
- protect individuals from the abuse of state power;
- further the economic and social policies of the state.

Law (and more particularly the machinery of law making) is, therefore, the principal vehicle for collective (rather than individual) change and collective enforcement. Lawyers, *qua* lawyers, are not overtly concerned with the qualitative nature of the rules surrounding particular issues, or indeed with legal rules in general. Qualitative matters (that is the creation and formulation of policy) are for society as a whole to consider, using the normal democratic and political processes for engendering change. The legal process is largely concerned with the drafting and interpretation of rules, together with enforcement.

The furtherance of economic and social policies requires a legal framework in order to create the organizational means by which to create change. Once the organizational means are in place, a legal framework is also necessary to ensure conformity by the use of sanctions (or more optimistically, by the threat of sanctions), that is, by an element of coercion. The popular notion of a legal rule is that of a command (usually delineated in legal terms by the word *shall*) backed by a sanction, the nature of which being dependent on the command in question. The rules of the criminal law, for example, often contain such sanctions as fines or imprisonment. Non-criminal sanctions may include the payment of damages and, in the case of special educational needs, court orders compelling local education authorities to reconsider decisions taken (see later: judicial review). The above definition is not always satisfactory and continues to be the subject of much debate. For instance, many legal rules relating to the work of local authorities are couched in terms of powers, where the word *may* is employed. Powers are discretionary rather than mandatory. None the less, the notion does serve to remind us that legal change normally requires an element of uniform coercion in order to succeed.

There are two main sources of law in the UK: case law and statute law. In the modern age, where parliamentary intervention has tended to predominate, case law (often alternatively known as judge-made law, precedent or common law) still retains its importance where, for example, legislation does not exist to deal with a particular issue coming before the courts, or where statute confers an element of discretion on the judiciary to build up a body of precedent. It is, however, in the field of statutory interpretation that the law-making powers of the courts are at their most evident – the interpretation of statutory rules in practice. We look to Acts of Parliament to bring about major change in the modern age. When a new bill is presented to Parliament and it is formally read for the first time, it already has a history, and its progress towards the statute-book is often fraught with argument and compromise. The agonies and ecstasies of the passing of the Education Act 1944 have been illuminatingly described in Lord Butler's (1971) autobiography.

There are a number of principal reasons why Parliament legislates:

- to give effect to the policies which the government was elected to carry out;
- to repeal and/or reform existing legislation;
- to consolidate legislation;
- to respond to matters of public concern;
- to consider bills (draft laws) presented to them.

Another fundamental question to ask at this stage is where do the policies come from? The simple answer is, from groups or sectors within society as a whole – pressure groups within and outside parliament voice concern and seek change. The journey from voicing concern to actually bringing about change is a long one. Policies must first gain the ear and the approval of the government of the day. Without this they will disappear without trace, however worthy the cause. Policy will then be subjected to a lengthy process of enquiry (often using the vehicle of the commission, parliamentary select committee or other form of public enquiry), public debate and continuing refinement (normally co-ordinated by the relevant government department) and thence through to a firm policy which is normally backed by the government of the day. This finalized policy will then appear as a White Paper, which is intended to set out the government's final views. From this, a draft bill will appear – ready to enter the parliamentary legislative process with an expectation (not always realized) of eventual adoption in law. White Papers are also consultation documents in the sense that comments are invited upon their contents within a specified period, but at this stage there is less likelihood that the government will be prepared to alter the basic principles of its policies, although matters of detail will still be open to debate. Once the consultation period for the White Paper has expired, the government, through its departments and parliamentary counsel will prepare a final version of the bill which will be laid before Parliament by the appropriate minister. The first step in this process is the publication of a Green Paper by the government. This is the first opportunity for the general public and interested bodies to participate formally in the policy-making process. It is an intermediate stage and may be omitted in order to save time. Green Papers are, essentially, discussion documents and their purpose is to promote public debate before the government firms up on its policies. Comments are invited from interested persons and bodies within a specified period.

The drafting of legal rules is a complex exercise. Although in recent years significant steps have been taken to simplify the wording of legislation (cf. the Children Act 1989), complexity (often inevitable) remains. Analyse for a moment a so-called 'simple' rule:

You must not kill; if you do kill, you will be killed.

The fact that the rule conforms to the definition introduced above, in that it contains a command and a sanction, becomes almost irrelevant when the meaning comes to be carefully considered:

- Kill what? A human being? What does that term mean? (Think of the rules relating to abortion, for example.)
- Killed by whom?
- Killed how?

None of these matters is trivial if an individual stands accused of a breach of the rule, and each element needs careful attention by way of definition.

Definitions themselves are either formulated by members of groups seeking to bring about change or, perhaps more haphazardly, by parliamentary draftsmen, attempting to lend clarity to a particular issue. Certainty of meaning is the objective, however imperfect the result may sometimes be.

Legislation in the modern age is often accompanied by other documentation of equal importance:

(1) *Statutory instruments/Orders in Council.* Statutes often contain 'enabling sections' within them, allowing for regulations of an

administrative nature to be made, enabling statement of general principle to be translated into practice.

(2) *Circulars*. Usually provided by departments of state, these contain guidance and explanatory material concerning what is generally considered to be good practice.

(3) *Codes of practice*. Again containing guidance and explanatory material, these may either be produced by departments of state or by professional bodies.

A final thought before tracing the statutory progress to date in relation to children with special needs is that many policies formulated to bring about change frequently become the victim of compromise during the legislative process. Deals are struck, factions are appeased and resourcing issues often lurk in the background. In many instances, bills entering parliament often appear to have more teeth in the form of duties than is the case with the final result – the Act of Parliament.

Law reform, therefore, is frequently a matter of the continuous refinement of existing legislation.

The legislation
The Education Act 1944
This established the framework for the education of children with disabilities which operated until the new legislation of the Education Act 1981. Prior to the 1944 Act, four categories of handicap were identified for which local education authorities (LEAs) had a duty to provide special schools and classes – blind, deaf, epileptic, and physically and mentally defective. The 1944 Act defined ten categories for which provision would normally be made in special schools – blind, partially sighted, deaf, partially deaf, delicate, educationally subnormal, epileptic, maladjusted, physically handicapped, and speech defects. There was, however, no requirement on local education authorities to educate children with these disabilities in special schools, but the Act suggested that 'the arrangements may provide for the giving of such education in any school maintained or assisted by the LEA'.

A further category of children, those who following a medical examination were judged to be 'ineducable', were the responsibility of the health authority. The Education Act 1970 removed the LEA's powers to classify such children as unsuitable for school and the responsibility for such children was transferred to the LEA. Junior training centres for the most part became schools for severely educationally subnormal children. Children in the educationally subnormal category formed by far the largest group and to provide for these children in particular the expansion of special schooling progressed steadily in the twenty or so years following the 1944 Act, even though in 1946 the government had envisaged that the majority of these children might be educated in ordinary schools.

Reservations, however, about the legislation and the practice became increasingly prevalent: the ten categories of handicap were seen as of little use in describing the needs of the children, and since children suffer from varying degrees of disability the labels themselves were difficult to apply. The concentration on the handicap, following the medical model of assessment rather than on the child's needs in an educational context, was also questioned. Recognizing these concerns, and given the wider trends which saw the opportunities for the handicapped reduced when segregated from the mainstream of society, the government set up the committee of enquiry chaired by Mary Warnock.

The Education Act 1981

This gave legislative effect to the central recommendation in the report of the Warnock Committee in 1978 (*Special Educational Needs*, Cmnd 7212) with the result that, instead of defined categories of handicap, children have 'special educational needs' if they have a learning difficulty which calls for special educational provision to be made for them (Education Act 1981, s.1 (1)). The Warnock Report estimated that up to 20 per cent of schoolchildren might have special educational needs requiring some additional provision at some stage during their school careers.

As stated above, children have 'special educational needs' if they have a learning difficulty which calls for special education provision to be made for them (s.1 (1)).

Children have a 'learning difficulty' if, *inter alia*:

- they have a significantly greater difficulty in learning than the majority of children of their age, or
- they have a disability which prevents or hinders them from making use of educational facilities of a kind generally provided in schools, within the area of the local education authority concerned, for children of their age.

(s. 1 (2))

For a pupil whose mother tongue is not English, by virtue of s. 1(4), the child's lack of competence in English is not a learning difficulty (DES, 1989a, Circular 22/89, para. 5).

Special educational provision, defined in s. 1(3), is additional to or different from the educational provision made generally for children of the same age by the local education authority. It can be made in ordinary school classes, by separate teaching, in a special unit forming part of an ordinary school, or otherwise. For children under the age of two, it is educational provision of any kind.

We have seen that a circular gives advice about good practice. Hence, DES Circular 22/89 states:

> The extent to which a learning difficulty hinders a child's development does not depend solely on the nature and severity of that difficulty. Other significant factors include the personal resources and attitudes of the child as well as the help and support provided at home and the provision made by the school, the LEA and other statutory and voluntary agencies. A child's special educational needs are thus related both to the abilities and disabilities and to the school and the extent of the interaction of these with his or her environment.
>
> (DES, 1989a, Circular 22/89)

Special educational needs is a concept capable of significant differing interpretation, but the intention of the 1981 Act, that the child's needs should be considered in context and not in isolation, was intended to be the central focus when the issues of formal assessment, making of statement and the provision of additional resources are being considered.

The LEA also has to identify those children whose needs require provision which it can only offer on an individual basis, whether in the child's school or in a special school or with other support. For such a decision, a multiprofessional assessment of the child must be carried out by LEA-designated personnel, with the needs and provision to be set out in a 'statement' which is required to be reviewed annually (s. 5 and s. 7).

According to DES Circular 22/89, para. 15 (DES, 1989a), since the implementation of the 1981 Act attention has tended to focus on the 2 per cent of the school population who have statements under s. 7, in some areas drawing attention away from the larger group, for whom none the less local educational authorities and school governors have duties under the Act. Up to 1981 it appeared to have been assumed that about 2 per cent of those who were at school were so disabled that they must receive special education in special schools.

> A different sort of education altogether with different goals could then be given to the remaining 98% of children who were normal . . . It began to be seen (however) that there were far more children than the 2% in special schools who had educational needs for which a school ought to lay on something special if their needs were to be met. The 1981

Education Act incorporated these ideals. They were not realised in practice (though the Act had considerable influence).

(Warnock, 1991)

The Children Act 1989

Monitoring, assessment and review of progress have to be seen as parts of a continuous process. The Children Act 1989, like the 1981 Act, clearly defines the need for communication between teachers, the school health service and social services departments (SSDs) as well as between the LEA and SSDs at a senior management level. Assistance before a situation becomes critical is more effective than formal assessment procedures initiated too late and in isolation. The needs of some children will be first identified while they are living with their family. Statutory assessments under s. 5 of the 1981 Act may sometimes be required for children who are living in provision made by the local authority such as foster placements, residential care homes or whilst placed in an independent school for primary residential care needs.

When the LEA notifies the parent of its decision to assess formally a child's special educational needs, a copy of the notification must be sent to an officer nominated for this purpose by the SSD. This is intended to offer the SSD an opportunity to consider whether they know of any problems affecting the child relevant to that authority and the range of services it might offer and to indicate to the LEA whether the social services have information relevant to the assessment of the child's special educational needs. Any advice provided by the SSD will be attached as an appendix to the statement. Parents have a right to see such advice. The LEA may also seek advice from the SSD of its own accord.

The notification of SSDs by LEAs may be an important opportunity for the SSD to meet with and inform parents of children in need with disabilities at a very early stage and to provide information about available services. This notification offers one of the few formal bridges between the two authorities and is an opportunity to link educational assessment to the assessment of a wider range of personal, social or health needs. It also demonstrates how the 1981 Act is extended and elaborated by subsequent legislation in the 1989 Act.

Parental involvement

Parents have rights to participation in assessment and subsequent special educational provision under the 1981 procedures. They see all copies of any professional advice made with regard to the assessment; they may contribute their own written comments on their child's special needs and their preferences and they have rights of appeal to a local appeals tribunal if they are unhappy with the outcome of the assessment. However, some parents do not participate as fully as they might in assessment without support. In some instances, particularly where the family has a range of needs unrelated to the educational assessment, SSDs or voluntary organizations may support parents in assessment. When a child is subject to a care order, the local authority should also ensure that it involves anybody with parental responsibility for the child in any assessment procedure (supporting them in travelling to an assessment if necessary), and act as a good parent, contributing positively to assessment and encouraging the child or young person to do likewise. Every statement of special educational needs must be reviewed annually. If there is anxiety concerning the arrangements made for the child, then reassessment may be requested.

Integration

Finally, both the Education Act 1981 and the Children Act 1989 place emphasis upon the importance of integration within mainstream provision for children with special needs wherever possible. Every effort should, therefore, be made to ensure that children can attend an ordinary local school. The linkage of assessment processes under the two parallel pieces of legislation is clearly a high priority if effectiveness and efficiency are to improve.

Education Reform Act 1988

The Education Reform Act 1988 is considered by many to have driven a wedge between the laudable intentions of the 1981 Act (as echoed and reinforced by the Children Act) and their effectiveness in practice. Reference to special educational needs is scant in the Act, but the central elements of the legislation relate to the funding of schools which depends predominantly on the number of pupils. Schools generally must compete for pupil numbers on the basis of their position in league tables of aggregate achievement in the National Curriculum. The potential disincentive for schools to admit pupils with special educational needs is clear, particularly given that LEA budgets have been reduced by Community Charge capping, loss of funds allocated to 'opted-out' grant-maintained schools and cut-backs in monies available for central services to support pupils with special educational needs.

The trend, resulting from the 1988 legislation, is reflected in increases in the percentage of pupils with statements of special needs in LEAs. If schools cannot resource need through the normal channels, the statement procedure provides a mechanism by which resources may be obtained from LEAs. A survey carried out at the Institute of Education (Lunt and Evans, 1991) found that 50 per cent of LEAs reported an overall increase in pupils placed in special schools, and a

Department for Education Report (DfE, 1992) expressed concern about the number of pupils with statements who were excluded from schools.

The complaints procedure and case law

Now we shall see how statute law is affected and modified by case law. According to statute, briefly stated, a parent's rights of appeal include:

- to the Secretary of State under s. 5 (6) of the 1981 Act when the LEA, having assessed the child, decides that it is not required to determine the special educational provision that should be made for him;
- to an appeal committee under s. 8 (2) against the LEA's proposed special educational provision that should be made for him;
- to the Secretary of State under s. 8 (6) against an appeal committee's decision, or against the LEA's decision where an appeal committee has remitted the case to the LEA for reconsideration;
- to the governing body under s. 19 (7) of the 1988 Act against a decision of the headteacher made under s. 19;
- against a decision of a governing body or the LEA, using the LEA's statutory complaints procedure under s. 23 of the 1988 Act;
- an application to the Secretary of State to give directions to an LEA or a governing body under powers conferred by ss. 68 and 99 of the Education Act 1944, but only after a complaint under s. 23 of the 1988 Act has been disposed of;
- an application for judicial review to the courts on the grounds of error of law, unreasonableness or breach of natural justice or unfairness; this course of action is increasingly likely to be pursued (see later);
- complaints may be made to the Commission for Local Administration in England (the local government ombudsman) in cases of alleged maladministration.

When a parent, child or other interested person asserts that the local authority is in breach of its statutory duty under the Education Act 1981 in relation to children with special educational needs, the Parents' Charter (Children with Special Needs) seeks to provide a simple guide to the ways in which parents may seek redress in circumstances where local authorities are demonstrating reluctance in meeting their children's needs. However, the charter has been roundly criticized by the Independent Panel for Special Educational Advice (IPSEA) for its errors and omissions. The Court of Appeal in the case of *E.* (see below) appreciated the valuable assistance of a flow chart in order to demonstrate the labyrinthine procedures under the Education Act 1981, whereas the Department of Education and Science (DES) publication which purports to set out a parent's rights and responsibilities under the 1981 Act is beguilingly simplistic.

Among many criticisms of the charter, perhaps the most significant is the omission to mention the right of a parent under s. 7 (4) (*b*) of the 1981 Act to require the LEA to arrange a meeting with an officer of the authority to discuss a proposed statement of a child's special educational needs. This is clearly an important opportunity for parents to explain their problem fully. It also appears finally to abandon one of the central ideas of the Warnock Report, that of the 'named person' to whom a parent may apply for support and information.

If a parent decides to appeal against the decision of an LEA, the first difficulty is that, even if the parent is successful in gaining the approval of the local appeal committee, the decision of the committee is not binding on the LEA. The second difficulty is that a further appeal to the Secretary of State can take up to twelve months to decide, and in the meantime the status quo will be maintained.

Case law
Alternatively, the parent may attempt to bypass the appeals procedure by applying directly for judicial review in the hope of establishing 'case law'. In cases involving children with special educational needs under the Education Act 1981 there is a steady flow of 'grey area' decisions by LEAs going against the parent. The parent in these circumstances has a stark choice – either to accept the decision, however reluctantly, or appeal against the decision. The decision to appeal is not one to be taken lightly in view of the complexity and time-consuming nature of the statutory process.

To recap: under the Education Act 1981, a child has special educational needs if he or she has a learning difficulty requiring special educational provision. The local education authority must identify children in its area who have such needs and assess them. If the authority concludes that special educational provision is not required, the parent may appeal to the Secretary of State, who may direct the local education authority to reconsider. Where the authority decides that such provision is required, it must make and maintain a statement of the child's needs – s. 7 and Schedule 1. Even where the authority decides that the child has special educational needs, if it believes such needs can be satisfied in an ordinary school it is not obliged to make a statement. I will discuss this by reference to a number of cases which have been influential in changing or clarifying the law.

In the first case,[1] the mother of a child with learning difficulties appealed against the refusal of her application for judicial review of the decision of the

LEA not to make a statement under s. 7. It was agreed that the child had special educational needs which the authority believed could be adequately dealt with in a remedial class of an ordinary school. The parent contended that the authority had thereby determined the special educational provision that should be made for the child and was, therefore, obliged to make a statement under s. 7.

It was held that an authority was not required by s. 7 to maintain a statement for every child with special educational needs; it was to do so only if of the opinion that it should determine the special educational provision that should be made for the child. Section 5 referred to a child having or probably having special educational needs which called for the authority to determine the special educational provision that should be made for him. That could not apply to every child who had, or probably had, such needs. From the wording of those sections it was plain that an authority had a discretion whether or not it should itself determine the special educational provision for a particular child with special educational needs or would leave the determination to others. Where, as in the present case, the decision as to what was to be done for the child was left to the school, it was not a determination by the authority itself under s. 7. Consequently it was not obliged to make a statement under that section.

This decision has been afforded further support by the second case,[2] where it was held that after making an assessment of a child's special educational needs under s. 5 of the Act and thereafter issuing a draft statement of his or her special educational needs, a local education authority was not obliged to go on to issue a final statement of special educational needs under s. 7.

On a more positive note, perhaps the greatest legal milestone offering an opportunity to further the special-needs cause came in 1991 in the third case to be discussed here.[3] This decision in favour of a child with learning difficulties has resource implications for local education authorities and schools, and was immediately welcomed by the Independent Panel for Special Educational Advice with a threat of further legal action to ensure that, when assessing the extent of children's special needs, local education authorities will take full account of the advice of educational psychologists. The facts of the case were these.

E., a bright and intelligent boy of thirteen, had learning difficulties that could be grouped under the headings of dyslexia and dyscalculia. Part II of the local education authority's statement dealing with his needs specified that he 'was experiencing difficulty with literacy and numeracy skills'. Part III of the statement dealt with special educational provisions for the literacy difficulties but did not mention his numeracy ones and stated that his local school was considered appropriate to provide for his needs.

E.'s parents took the view that specialized education at a boarding school fifty-five miles from their home was required. *E.* had been attending that school since 1987 and the substantive issue which lay behind the case was whether Dorset County Council should be required to meet the expense.

Being dissatisfied with the special educational provision specified in Part III of the statement, *E.*'s parents appealed to the Secretary of State under s. 8 (6) of the Act (that is, according to statute).

In his letter dismissing their appeal, the Secretary of State said that he was satisfied that the provision specified in Part III, which included additional specialist teaching for reading and spelling, would adequately meet the needs described in Part II of the statement.

The parents, on behalf of *E.*, then applied for judicial review of the Secretary of State's decision. The judge held that if the numeracy difficulty was serious enough to appear in the LEA's statement, then that difficulty necessarily qualified for special educational provision under the 1981 Act and reg. 10 of the Education (Special Educational Needs) Regulations 1983 (SI 1983 No. 29), and therefore quashed the Secretary of State's decision. This new decision was upheld on appeal.

The Department of Education and Science acted quickly to get this decision widely known and acted upon by issuing SEN Letter 91/1. That letter to chief education officers said that

> the purpose in writing to you is to set out the main implications of the judgement. The judgement makes clear that once a local education authority have decided that they are required to determine that some special educational provision should be made for a child they must maintain a statement of special educational needs for him. The LEA must set out, in Part II of the child's statement, all of his special educational needs as assessed under s. 5 of the Education Act 1981. They must also specify, in Part III, the special educational provision that should be made for each and every one of those needs.

This extract clearly signals much more of a commitment to make adequate provision for children with special educational needs, and represents a considerable departure from the tenor of the judgement in a previous case[4] which concerned whether a child should go to a special school:

> There is no question of Parliament having placed the local authority under an obligation to provide a child with the best possible education. There is no duty on the authority to provide such a Utopian system, or to educate him to his maximum potential.

That is undoubtedly a correct statement of the law, but until the case of *E.* it might have been relied upon by some LEAs as authority for the proposition that the LEA could not be expected to do more than the budget allows. Now, in the case of *E.*, we have the Court of Appeal's ruling interpreted by the DES as a requirement that the LEA must, for every 'statemented' child, prescribe for each and every one of the child's needs. Thus case law has again clarified statute.

Although the case of *E.* has provided a signpost by way of assisting parents to assert their rights successfully, litigation under the Act is in fact increasing. In January 1993 it was reported that two test cases which were currently before the High Court were described as the first examples of parents suing for 'educational negligence'. The cases are both centred around the 1981 Act and involve Dorset and Hampshire local education authorities. Both actions are for damages following what the plaintiffs allege were the failures of the authorities to recognize cases of dyslexia.

The parents of a fourteen-year-old boy are suing Dorset LEA for compensation for some 30,000 of private school fees they claim they were forced to pay because the local authority was unable to provide special-needs education. More alarmingly, Hampshire is being sued by a man for loss of earnings. Here the plaintiff claims he was provided with an inadequate education because educational psychologists at the LEA did not recognize the severity of his dyslexia. If damages are awarded in either or both of these cases, there are others waiting in the wings.

In the last five or six years the number of applications for judicial review under the Act has risen from ten to twenty annually to approximately 120 applications in 1992. It has been suggested that there are two principal reasons for such an increase:

- the availability of legal aid to children;
- increased parental awareness of a possible remedy. This is considered to be a direct result of the consumerist 1980s where people were led to believe that they had rights which they could enforce. At the forefront of this movement is a volunteer group known as the Independent Panel for Special Educational Advice. Founded in 1983, its primary aim is to provide free second opinions to parents regarding LEA reports on a child's educational needs. In 1992 IPSEA dealt with about 900 enquiries which required some level of advice. Of those, about 80 per cent involved parents querying whether an LEA had fulfilled its duties under the 1981 Act, and in about half of these cases there was reason to believe the LEA was in breach of its statutory obligation.

Proposals for reform
The Centre for Studies on Integration in Education (CSIE) in May 1992 designated a National Integration Week and drafted legislation 'to make

provision for the inclusion of all children regardless of race, class, religion, disability, learning difficulty or emotional needs, within one, mainstream, education system', thus emphasizing the recommendation of the Warnock Committee that so far as possible children with special educational needs should be integrated into ordinary schools. CSIE would also give a final power to an appeal committee to bind the LEA.

The various proposed amendments to the 1981 Act also reflect the view of the Education Law Association (ELAS) that children with learning difficulties and their parents need legal and other professional advice when faced by LEAs which are desperate to conserve resources. Educational psychologists in particular require professional courage to state fully the special educational needs of children, regardless of the resource implications for their employers, the LEAs. It has been alleged that pressure from the LEA has led professional advisers, such as educational psychologists, to fail to state the full extent of children's learning difficulties and special needs, due to resource implications. There has been an informed prediction that educational psychologists will be sued for negligence. The judgements in the case of *E.* have fuelled a controversy as to whether LEAs take available resources as their starting point and, simply by ignoring their statutory duties, tailor assessments of a child to the authority's resources.

There is also a growing concern that pupils are not being admitted to or are being excluded from schools on disciplinary grounds, when in fact the child has a problem which requires special educational provision for which neither the LEA nor the school (managing its own budget) accepts responsibility.

Education Act 1993

As mentioned in the introduction to this chapter, legislative reform frequently concerns the refinement of existing legislation. The Education Act 1993 attempts to deal, at least in part, with some of the issues and abuses voiced by an increasing number of people. Part III of the Act re-enacts virtually the whole of the 1981 Act and legislates for the proposals contained in the White Paper and the separate DfE consultation document on special education needs: *Access to the System*. The major issues are:

- Section 149, which rewrites s. 7 of the 1981 Act and includes a requirement for a school that is named in a statement to admit the child. The section also requires the same school to be consulted prior to the statement being made. Schedules 8 and 9 contain powers for the Secretary of State to make regulations about the timescale for the assessment and statementing processes. The right of appeal against an LEA decision to cease to maintain a statement is to be introduced.

- Section 150 allows a parent to appeal against a decision not to make a statement (a key element of current complaint), and s. 151 allows for an appeal against the contents of a statement.
- Section 154 allows the governing body of a grant-maintained school to require that a child be assessed.
- Sections 157–61 deal with the Special Educational Needs Tribunal to which parents can appeal at various stages of the assessment and statementing process. This replaces the present local independent appeal committees and appeals to the Secretary of State. The tribunal will consist of a president and two panels, one panel containing legally qualified persons who can serve as chairpersons of tribunals, and the other containing people who can serve as the other two members of each tribunal. No qualifications are required of people in this second panel, which is described as a 'lay panel'. The DfE consultation statement stated that this panel would consist of people who had knowledge of local government administration and special educational provision. Section 160 allows regulations to be made about the proceedings of the tribunal including holding of hearings in private, granting of the right of discovery or inspection of documents, requiring persons to attend and give evidence under oath. Schedule 9 allows, on appeal, the tribunal to dismiss the appeal or order the LEA to add the name of the school for which the parent expressed a preference to the statement or to substitute that name for the name of the school specified in the statement.

For all the largely procedural reforms envisaged by the 1993 Act, there are a number of important concerns which are currently being voiced in relation to pupils with special needs. In particular:

(1) The integration of pupils with special educational needs into ordinary schools may be further hindered if the cost of meeting those needs is part of the school's normal budget.
(2) Competition for pupil numbers, introduced by the 1988 Act, is re-emphasized in the new legislation. Additional expenditure required for special education needs may not, therefore, be seen as an ideal way of maximizing resources.

Conclusions
There is . . . a bleak consequence of the market-led concept of education and that is the inescapable fact that in the market-place some are losers. Some schools, we are told, will simply turn out to be

too bad, and will either have to improve or close. But what if such a 'bad' school fails to come up with the proper examination results because it has a lot of 'bad' pupils who cannot pass examinations? What will happen to such pupils in the future? We are already told that schools may 'exempt' certain pupils from the National Curriculum tests. There is a real danger that such pupils may also be 'exempted' from the National Curriculum itself.

(Warnock, 1991, p. 151)

If the proposals for reform contained in the Education Act 1993, particularly in relation to the Special Educational Needs Tribunal, mean that the legal rights of parents and children are credibly enhanced to a point where the assessment and provision of special educational need takes place in a significantly larger percentage of cases, and takes place more effectively and efficiently than hitherto, there may be other matters of a 'discriminatory' nature which neither the amended Education Act 1981 nor the Children Act 1989 necessarily envisage. As was discussed earlier, there appeared to have been a general consensus between 1944 and the 1980s that everyone was entitled to the best, or if they could not get the best they were entitled to a chance of it. An assumption of equal entitlement to education within a global concept of meeting educational needs does not necessarily remain equal entitlement if performance indicators for defining success and quality are biased against the notion and, therefore, fail to encourage the concept. The last decade or so in relation to special educational needs, when considered from the point of view of legal rights, may be remembered for its slow and somewhat negative beginnings in case law to more radical change initiated by the courts and subsequently underpinned by parliament. Such interpretations, adjustments and changes to the original 1981 blueprint have concerned compliance with that blueprint in relation to improved opportunity for assessment and acknowledgement of special educational need. If recent reforms mean anything, they should reflect a greater degree of compliance. Whether equality of opportunity within the same school then becomes a reality may be quite another matter.

This chapter has attempted to demonstrate the way education policy was shaped by statute and case law. No doubt the Education Act 1993 will be clarified, amended and changed by case law in the same way. It is hoped that this will increase rather than decrease the opportunities for children with special educational needs.

Notes

(1) *R. v. Secretary of State for Education and Science ex parte Lashford* (1988) 1FLR 72.

(2) R. v. *Isle of Wight County Council ex parte S* (1992) *The Times*, 2 November.

(3) R. v. *Secretary of State for Education and Science ex parte E*. (1991) *The Independent*, 9 May.

(4) R. v. *Surrey County Council Education Committee ex parte H*. (1984) 83 LGR 219 CA.

For the reader
To clarify your own understanding of the law, look up the Acts of Parliament in your library and decide for yourself how successful the legislation has been for the children you teach. Has case law had any demonstrable effect on practice as you experience it?

3

A Testing Time for Psychologists

Carol Aubrey

Since the explicit intention of this book is to consider special educational needs (SEN) from a range of perspectives, I intend first to review the concept of special need in the current educational context, next to consider the implications of this for the psychologist and, finally, to assess what role the psychologist might have for the rest of the 1990s.

In April 1993 it was ten years since the Education Act 1981 came into force. It is now timely to consider how the Act has been implemented and the extent to which things have changed. I make no apology for using this decade as the context for examining the concept of special educational need since our terminology and our whole frame of reference is rooted in the late 1970s and the 1980s and originated in the Warnock Report of 1978. This provided special educators with an unchallenged ideology, even a moral imperative: 'Integration is "the central contemporary issue in special education"' (DES, 1978, p. 79). Such values and beliefs about special education have been so widely shared that in order to consider this period critically one must first clarify the nature of common underlying assumptions, in order to access what has become almost taken for granted.

For a decade Warnock's framework has provided a powerful model. It has one key concept: the concept of 'educational need' defined in terms of what each child will need to make progress. This she has recently described in the following terms: 'Schools could be presumed to supply what most children needed; special provision would be required if others were to progress, sometimes, provision of a temporary kind. [The] . . . overriding concern was to ensure that these needs could be not only identified, but met' (Warnock, 1992a, p. 3).

Further, the idea of a continuum of special need, of ability and disability, was central.

We had a clear picture of all children tramping along a common educational road, towards a common destination of enhanced enjoyment, independence and responsibility, but encountering along the way obstacles of different degrees of severity. Our aim was to show that there was a continuum of difficulty in those obstacles but that children could be helped over them one by one and their progress measured by how far along the common road they could get.

(ibid)

The government's White Paper *Choice and Diversity* (DES, 1992b), together with the report *Getting the Act Together* and the ensuing document *Getting in on the Act* produced by the Audit Commission and HMI (1992a, 1992b), has offered serious criticisms of special education presently available to children. Wide-ranging changes have been recommended which will help to clarify the law and to ensure that both schools and local authorities can be held accountable for Warnock's 18 per cent, those vulnerable children without a statement. In line with this, new proposals made for children with SEN in the Education Act 1993 are little different from those contained in the White Paper. In addition, the government intends to establish national guidelines for statements of special need and to speed up the assessment procedures. Special needs will remain one of the few responsibilities left with local authorities if, as the government hopes, grant-maintained schools become the norm. Local authorities will retain responsibility for assessing and issuing statements and will be given a new power to tell grant-maintained schools to take pupils excluded from other institutions and to name grant-maintained schools on school attendance orders (subject to appeal by the governors). The governors may also require the local authority to assess any of these pupils to see whether a statement of SEN is needed. The current appeals system is to be replaced with a new special-needs tribunal.

Who then has overall responsibility for special education? While local authorities maintain responsibility for the 2 per cent or so children with statements, who will support the 18 per cent? Already there are signs that local authorities are beginning to make cuts as financial delegation to schools is established. The news section of *Special Children* for February 1993, entitled 'Job losses begin to gather pace', asserted that 'Cash-starved local authorities are making special needs support staff and educational psychologists redundant in a desperate attempt to balance their books' (*Special Children*, 1993, p. 5). The article suggested that a number of local authorities were currently carrying out a restructuring aimed at streamlining services as funding was transferred to schools. There are clear signs that under the economic constraints of the late 1980s resulting from changes in roles and financial responsibilities accruing from the Education Reform Act 1988, as well as from the effects of major economic recession, the much vaunted 'spirit of Warnock' is evaporating.

Governmental criticism of current special education was first made manifest in a House of Lords debate towards the end of 1991. Concern was raised that the Education Act 1981 was not being implemented properly. To use Warnock's own recent comments, 'in spirit it was incompatible with the 1988 Education Act and in any case it was flawed' (ibid).

The instigator and originator of this reform and arch representative of the Establishment, Baroness Warnock herself, was in the process of dismantling the special educational system and dispelling associated beliefs which had dominated the last decade. The whole basis for special education, upon which the legal framework and administrative arrangements had been precariously erected, was being demolished.

As Sutton (1992) observed, 'In special education as in the rest of our education system it is now Open Season on Holy Cows'. But Warnock's own words were, perhaps, more surprising:

> The report was naive to the point of idiocy. We were deeply enamoured of our own ideals (perhaps infatuated would be a better word). The idea of the continuum is too vague . . . We invented an elaborate system by which the most severely handicapped children were to be statemented. The whole concept of statementing for only a few children with the rest supposedly having their needs met according to what individual schools can provide must be rethought . . . What is needed is a radical revision of the way we assess children's educational needs and, far more important, how we can then be confident these needs are going to be met . . . this is the more urgent as schools become increasingly competitive over examination results and have to manage their own finances . . . LEAs are increasingly drawing up statements not in accordance with the child's needs but with what they think they can afford.
>
> (Warnock, 1992a)

One would have to note, too, that these views were expressed after publication of the White Paper and the Audit Commission/HMI documents and, in fact, they added little new to the debate. It took a new educational and political context to bring to a head issues of financial management which clearly had been fudged in the original Education Act 1981. Despite the stridency of the criticisms made (and Warnock was willing to accept the empirical evidence which demonstrated the Act was not working), in view of her own academic background in philosophy, it is perhaps surprising that, as is the case for Professor Anthony O'Hear with respect to criticisms of primary education, she does not really bring to bear a rigorous philosophical analysis of fundamental concepts of her own creation. This means that her assumption that SEN forms a continuum, from mild and temporary to major and lasting, and her definition of special educational need in terms of educational provision remains unchallenged.

The writer's intention at this point is to consider critically the concepts upon which our current special educational system is founded and the extent to which empirical evidence is available to substantiate them.

The concepts
First of all the notion of the continuum of need, as Warnock said at the time:

> We have been concerned, however, not only with the severely handicapped but with all those children who require special education in any form. The help may range from continuous support from specialist services, including an intensive educational programme in a special school for a child with severe and multiple difficulties, to part-time assistance from a specially trained teacher for a child with mild learning difficulties. It is perhaps useful to regard this range of special educational need as a continuum, although this is a crude notion which conceals the complexities of individual need.
>
> (DES, 1978, p. 6, para. 1.9)

The historical basis for this concept in an earlier psychometric tradition of special education has been analysed exhaustively elsewhere and in a number of different contexts, for instance Sutton (1981). Suffice it to say (and I quote here from some of my own writing dated 1986 which was never submitted for publication bearing in mind the spirit of the times):

> This 'crude notion' generally regarded (in its time) as humane in intent, in fact, by its stress on quantitative differences in learning difficulties on a continuum rather than qualitative differences, together with a coyness about specifying the nature of these difficulties, has led to confused thinking on the part of administrators, psychologists and parents alike, and provided as rigid a barrier to the appropriate management of the severely handicapped as the previous IQ score barriers of 50–55 between the moderately and severely handicapped.
>
> (Aubrey, 1986a, unpublished)

This apparently 'new' notion of a continuum was clearly derived from an earlier model of special education where decisions about special schooling were based on IQ cut-off points, 50–70 being the crude band from within which the old ESN (educationally subnormal) (moderate) group was selected and below which the ESN (severe) lay. I have described elsewhere (Aubrey, 1986b) how with the rise of compulsory education came a need to devise mechanisms (psychometric measurement with all the status of science) for identifying and making separate provision for those deemed through reason of learning or poor adjustment unfit to benefit from ordinary schooling. This happened in France with the work of Binet and in Great Britain a little later under the impetus of the work of Burt. Similar trends were in operation in the USA. Again, as can be demonstrated in the USA and Great Britain and, as I have documented with respect to France (Aubrey, 1987), the boundaries of mental retardation moved upwards to encompass a larger and larger group of children who were regarded as mildly retarded (see particularly, Netchine and Netchine, 1976). The effect was, and this has been extensively documented by Barton and Tomlinson (1981), for instance, that more and more minority children were labelled under the old system and found their way into special education. This culminated in a large extension of the provision for the ESN(M) and the so-called maladjusted groups in the 1960s and early 1970s, at the time the Warnock Committee was set up. So as we moved away from a system of categories of handicap with the Warnock Report (1978) and the ensuing Education Act 1981 to the blander and more 'politically correct' term of SEN, we kept the psychometric (IQ testing) origins in the notion of the continuum of learning difficulty (mild, moderate and severe). Within the notion of continuous differences with no qualitative differences among different handicaps acknowledged or their impact on learning and development appreciated, the concept of SEN was defined in educational terms as school provision required to meet the pupil's needs, or to 'encourage progress'.

In order to consider critically the possible flaws in our, then, liberal thinking about equal rights for the handicapped, integration and de-labelling or, at any rate, to consider the limits of its applicability, I turned to comparative education. This provided a means both of considering other kinds of cultural responses to similar phenomena and also of uncovering implicit assumptions about the nature of handicap left unexamined in our own context. In the unpublished manuscript (1986) referred to above I wrote:

> It is the writer's view that current special education ideology with no precise legal or administrative definition of handicap fails to:
> (i) separate problems of learning from problems of teaching, practically or conceptually;
> (ii) account for qualitative differences in learning of children, for instance, with known cerebral damage.
> (Aubrey, 1986a, unpublished)

A study of published professional literature by psychologists in France and Great Britain, undertaken in the year the Education Act 1981 came into force, allowed me to reflect on and make a comparison of our own current ideologies and practices with those of a close European partner. The aim of this study (Aubrey, 1986b) was to examine published professional communications by psychologists in France and Great Britain on the topical issue of integration. British psychologists, I found, secure in their central legal involvement in the assessment procedures of the new Education Act 1981 did not raise the integration of handicapped children in the ordinary school as an issue. A theme running through their professional literature was the incorporation of assessment/intervention-type procedures of applied behavioural models with the legal requirements of assessment/classification of children with special needs. Much concern was expressed by French psychologists, on the other hand, about two integration circulars of 1982 and 1983. They saw the circulars as affecting directly the conceptual framework within which they worked, the development of individual skills and their, perhaps, more precarious career prospects. In both contexts psychologists were preoccupied with their own professional practice and career security. The French psychologists, however, unlike their British counterparts, were also concerned to express their criticism of a lack of definition of handicap which they saw as reducing the child to a single scholastic dimension, and thus confusing psychology with pedagogy.

Empirical studies of the time

Concern of French psychologists about similar special educational concepts, with their accusation that the special child was reduced to a single scholastic dimension which confused psychology with pedagogy, points perhaps to the fundamental flaw in Warnock's thinking. Using her own approach of consulting empirical studies for the period, in fact, proved an illuminating exercise. Empirical evidence from the period in question is well summarized by a scholarly US review of Macmillan, Keogh and Jones (1986) of mildly handicapped learners. Their findings indicated that research had been directed less specifically to the problems of identification and teaching of handicapped children than towards legitimating special education policies already in force. A similar picture emerges from the scrutiny of British studies which also tended to concentrate on broad features of provision.[1] Thus educational settings and administrative arrangements, that is the place where children were receiving education, were regarded as a 'treatment' rather than the method by which they were taught. Whilst this permits conclusions to be drawn about the consequences of educational decision-making or the delivery of education services it fails to enlighten us much about how children are being taught in various settings. Interestingly it is precisely this information which the recent documents by the Audit Commission and HMI seek now to obtain through the increased accountability of schools and local authorities. We do, however, know much about the progress of mildly handicapped children who comprise the largest group of special children. I turn here, again, to a US research review (Reynolds, 1989). He suggested that whatever we choose to call these children they can be identified easily in the ordinary school setting because:

• they are not responding positively to the instruction offered in basic skills, e.g. reading;
• their social behaviour is unacceptable;
• they are falling behind in learning academic subjects;
• they may have significant physical limitations or major health problems;
• English is often not their first language;
• they are extremely limited in experiences which provide the background for formal education.

(Reynolds, 1989, p.130)

A similar pattern of findings with respect to the nature and extent of learning difficulties emerges from British research. Croll and Moses (1985) found that in 428 junior classrooms, teachers considered that 18.8 per cent of the 12,310 pupils had special educational needs. Whilst the three main categories overlapped, learning difficulties formed the core, the others being behaviour problems and health problems, including sensory and physical impairment. The Inner London Educational Authority (ILEA, 1986) carried out a four-year longitudinal study of nearly 2,000 children attending fifty junior schools. This showed marked differences in attainments between social groups, substantially lower reading attainments for pupils from minority ethnic groups who were not fluent in spoken English, as well as lower attainments for younger (summer-term born) children and boys as opposed to girls (on average five months of reading age).

In all cases the underlying characteristics are complex and beyond the full control of teachers and schools. The response of special-needs children to teaching is poor whatever the setting. Whilst they may be moved to special settings as a result of low achievement this feature persists across the contexts in which they may be placed. No teaching principles, however, which are uniquely applicable to special children have been identified for such groups. There is little evidence to support a need for qualitatively different forms of instruction. This suggests that such pupils usually need more teaching, not a different kind of teaching, than other pupils. An important, yet still relatively unexplored, development for SEN pupils is cognitive strategy training.

In line with current cognitive theory, learning of able and disabled pupils is seen as transformative rather than cumulative in nature and developed out of social interaction. Research from metacognition provides an empirical base for clarifying the learner's role in the learning process and the teaching of self-regulated behaviour. Brown and Campione (1986), for instance, have placed emphasis in teaching on strategies to be used to learn more effectively. In fact, learning disabled pupils can learn self-monitoring to increase on-task behaviour, for independence training, to control their own learning, to apply self-monitoring strategies, to evaluate performance or self-regulate when prompted (Ashman and Conway, 1989). Educational psychologists have shown a considerable interest in early models of cognitive strategy training, in particular instrumental enrichment (IE). Less attention has been paid to more recent applications which require detailed understanding of present knowledge, concepts and misconceptions held by pupils in particular subject fields and necessary transformations to be made by teachers to assist in gradually reshaping children's existing 'schemata' used to structure their view of the world (for example, Tharp and Gallimore's (1988) programme of assisted instruction in language, literacy and thinking for at-risk elementary school children).

Obviously such children must be treated individually but the challenge is to provide highly focused teaching rather than to allow delays to increase exponentially through the early years of school. Pupils who show limited progress in the early phases of instruction tend to show progressive retardation over succeeding years.

Systematic observation of such pupils' classroom experience shows it to be different from other children's. Whilst teachers spend twice as much time working with them individually, SEN children spend less time in groups and more time on individual tasks. They are involved in slightly lower levels of interaction as members of the class and lower levels of interaction in group work (Croll and Moses, 1985).

Turning now to the needs of the severely handicapped – and, again, using other cultural contexts to place in relief British practice – in contrast to Great Britain, some other parts of Europe are organized on different special educational principles and interpret integration differently. In France, for instance, as I have discussed elsewhere (Aubrey, 1987) the principle of integration by no means contradicts the requirement of differentiated special provision for the severely handicapped. The most favourable way of training mentally handicapped children towards as full an integration as possible in adult society may be to educate them in a special setting. Specific instruction for specific handicap is sought in different types of setting in accordance with the type or degree of defect and, if necessary, under conditions of differentiation. Similar goals pertain for the Hungarian conductive education method. Here structured training will aim at optimizing development with a view to integrating into ordinary schools where possible and, for those more severely disabled, eventual integration into society as an independent or semi-independent adult (Cottam and Sutton, 1986). Should we be too surprised if in integrated settings the needs of our most severely handicapped children were not being met? Have they gained qualitatively by being encompassed by a legislation and educational policy which incorporates a fully comprehensive range of our children? Given our present state of knowledge we must consider whether our present liberal thinking may risk our endeavours becoming as irrelevant, rigid and mechanical as ever they were before the present legislation was brought into operation.

Since the mid-1970s when the Warnock Report was first conceived, this country has been transformed socially, politically, economically and educationally. Now mechanisms from within, from the ruling classes themselves, are finally beginning to challenge the educational ideology which has dominated our thinking for more than a decade. This is more than a question of whether or not a statement will be modified or disapplied, or whether a child will receive education in an ordinary or special school. Perhaps it is time now to recognize the need for a clearer theoretical base for special education in this country.

The implications for the educational psychologist

What, then, has been the nature of educational psychologists' practice during this period? As described earlier in this chapter, the historical roots of psychological practice rest firmly within a tradition of psychometric measurement as the means of identifying, assessing, classifying and, sometimes, the basis for treating those pupils who are failing in ordinary schools. This is the expectation of the government and employers, at present the local education authority, as well as parents and teachers. Broader views of psychological practice must be justified in terms of development or refinement of existing methods and techniques of assessment and treatment of such pupils. With psychologists' statutory involvement in the statementing procedure assured and with a consequent increase in the number of psychologists employed, the rather loosely defined special education system provided a context for a very considerable broadening of and development in psychologists' knowledge base and professional practice. A more clearly delineated professional role for the psychologist as consultant was developed, drawing on mental health and US school psychology, as well as management consultancy literature (see Aubrey, 1988, 1990a, 1990b, 1992). The consultation model which distinguished between the development of process skills (interpersonal, relationship-building skills) and content skills (professional methods and practice) provided a new framework for an indirect service delivery where psychologists might work with parents and teachers, or provide whole-school and preventive approaches concerned as much with changing attitudes and behaviour of adults as with work concerning individual children. Such work drew increasingly on social, organizational and humanistic psychology as noted by Jones and Frederickson (1990). A similar shift in emphasis can be discerned in approaches to learning and behaviour which have stressed the development of higher-order competence in a complex social and physical environment, and which reflect advances in both educational and psychological research.

Turning to the empirical evidence related to psychological practice for the period an important source is an HM Inspectorate (HMI) report (DES, 1990a) which resulted from visits to one-third of services between Easter 1988 and summer 1989. As noted above, one result of the Education Act 1981 was an increase in general staffing in educational psychology services to an overall total in England of around 2,000, with staffing ratios ranging from one psychologist per 2,700 to one psychologist per 9,300 children of statutory age. The Warnock Report (1978), in fact, had recommended one psychologist to 5,000 children and young people up to the age of nineteen.

Working practice of all psychologists was affected by the Education Act 1981 but HMI observed that most obtained a reasonable balance between reactive and preventive work. Although less emphasis was being placed on traditional testing and reporting, assessment continued to be a major part of the psychologist's work. Statutory assessment, however, tended to arise naturally from less formal work related to learning and social adjustment already undertaken. Some services, HMI noted, were not providing the statutory requirement for reassessment of pupils aged thirteen years or more who were already statemented under the Education Act 1981. In terms of preventive work, there was an increasing emphasis on the provision of support and development for teachers and other professionals at both the individual and the institutional level.

Throughout this period the assumption has been that the psychologist as independent professional would offer an objective and unbiased view of children's needs without recourse to the consideration of resource implications or financial feasibility. As Gold (1991) noted, however, psychologists deal with children for whom normal resources are by current definition not enough. Their assessment can influence heavily the educational decision-making related to the future provision for the child in question. As resources diminish – as reported in the early part of this chapter – can psychologists ignore and have they, anyway, ignored the resource implications of their recommendations? To echo the main theme of this book: whose interests will they serve in this new climate of cost-effectiveness and professional accountability?

Private psychological services in general have acted as advocate for the family and child. In a time of impending service contraction where SEN budgets are increasingly devolved to schools two factors seem clear:

(1) With the recent increase in the number of requests for assessment under the statementing procedure, more and more of psychologists' time will be spent on statutory work.
(2) With increased accountability and value-for-money high on the agenda psychologists will have to demonstrate the value of their other, non-statutory work such as school training, the provision of parental advice, the monitoring of school-based interventions and individual counselling.

The Audit Commission/HMI (1992a) report *Getting in on the Act* recommended that psychologists should attend the annual review of every statemented pupil at least every two years. Bearing in mind the fact that HMI (DES, 1990a) had found that psychologists were not always even providing the statutory requirement of the thirteen-plus years statutory reassessment, an increased emphasis on statutory work seems inevitable. Whether or not psychologists will be involved in the development of SEN practice outlined in the second Audit Commission/HMI report (1992b), *Getting the Act Together*, is less clear.

What role for the future?
It is salutary to note that HMI (DES, 1990a) concluded that at this time of significant change in the educational system it was appropriate for educational psychology services to consider their future role. In fact applied psychologists, including educational psychologists, have been engaged in exploring the feasibility of introducing a new and acceptable framework of occupational standards at Level 5 of the National Council for Vocational Qualifications (NCVQ) to specify the nature of their work, their standards and qualifications (BPS, 1992). Under a general-purpose statement, to improve the educational/learning experience of children aged nought to nineteen through the direct and indirect application of psychological knowledge and skills, four main areas of work were identified. These were: (1) direct service to clients, (2) train and develop others, (3) provide an effective service, and (4) contribute to the development of the profession. Despite an overall positive response to the pilot study, concern about the applicability of the NCVQ approach to the

professional level was expressed, in particular the extent to which the framework could incorporate the assessment of the basic knowledge component in awarding professional qualifications, the degree to which the specification of competences could cover the range of professional work and whether assessment methods adopted could capture the essence of professional work.

Furthermore, it was concluded, that whilst appreciating that a shared perception of the skills being used and assessed was needed, the profession itself was in a much better position than its employers to specify the required competences. This, of course, leaves unanswered the question of whether or not a shared perception of the role and balance of areas (1) and (2) of the psychologist's work could be attained and whether the psychologist would be left to call the tune.

HMI (DES, 1990a) noted it was likely that psychologists would need to promote their services more readily in the future, that they would need to negotiate their role with local authority officers, teachers, parents and other professionals, incorporated and integrated with local authority policies and providing a positive and flexible response to changing demands. Finally they called for psychologists to appraise the frequency and extent to which their unique range of specialist skills were currently used, in particular, their knowledge of child development and learning processes. Could this knowledge be the more conventional educational psychology knowledge base of individual differences and could this be the call for a return to a more traditional, professional role?

With teachers themselves increasingly sophisticated in National Curriculum-based assessment for individual children, and special schools mapping their already sophisticated, developmentally appropriate curricula on to attainment targets, psychologists may be faced once more with the issues which first exercised the minds of their forerunners: how to devise tasks to identify those unable to benefit from the curriculum of ordinary schools for reasons related to learning and social adjustment.

After the Education Act 1981 psychologists, secure in their statutory role, felt free to extend their unique range of specialist skills. After the Education Act 1993 and subsequent changes to the statementing procedures, whilst still secure in their statutory role, psychologists may, in fact, be faced with a challenge to these newly acquired skills. Perhaps instead of building a new scientific basis for special education they will be required to rekindle a psychometric tradition which never really died with Warnock in the 1980s but was, instead, simply appropriated to serve a social, educational and political context which has now vanished.

Note

(1) After the passing of the Education Act 1981 a number of studies were set up to investigate the response of local authorities, for instance: (i) at the Institute of Education, University of London: Gipps, C., Gross, H. and Goldstein, H. (1987) *Warnock's Eighteen Percent of Children with Special Needs in Primary Schools*, The Falmer Press Lewes; Gross, H. and Gipps, C. (1987) *Supporting Warnock's Eighteen Percent: Six Case Studies*, The Falmer Press Lewes; Goacher, B. *et al.* (1988) *Policy and Provision for Special Educational Needs: Implementing the 1981 Education Act*, Cassell, London; (ii) at the National Foundation of Educational Research: Moses, D., Hegarty, S. and Jowett, S. (1988) *Supporting Ordinary Schools: LEA initiatives*, NFER-Nelson, Windsor; Jowett, S., Hegarty, S. and Moses, D. (1988) *Joining Forces: A Study of Links between Special and Ordinary Schools*, NFER-Nelson, Windsor; Hegarty, S. and Moses, D. (1988) *Developing Expertise: INSET for Special Needs*, NFER-Nelson, Windsor; (iii) at the University of Manchester: Robson, C., Sebba, J., Mittler, P. and Davies G. (1988) *In-Service Training and Special Educational Needs: Running Short School-Focused Courses*, Manchester University Press; DES-sponsored research: (iv) the Centre for Studies in Integration (CSIE), with Will Swann of the Open University, has analysed data supplied by the DfE related to local authorities' segregated and integrated SEN provision. Since the passing of the Education Reform Act 1988 the Institute of Education, University of London, the Centre for the Analysis of Social Policy, Bath University, and the NFER have monitored the delegation of financial management by local authorities with particular reference to SEN pupils.

For the reader

How would you define special educational need? What is the relative importance of where and how special needs will be met? What were the flaws of the Warnock Report (DES 1978) and the resultant Education Act 1981? Will the increased accountability of local authorities and schools recommended by *Getting in on the Act* (Audit Commission and HMI, 1992a) raise the standard of provision to which the most vulnerable children are entitled? What will be the role of the educational psychologist in this context?

Introduction to Chapters 4, 5, 6 amd 7

The next four chapters are concerned with a range of professional perspectives which are often grouped together under the aegis of medicine. However, as shall be seen, simply to talk of 'paramedical specialisms' is an inadequate description. The doctors themselves are considered in Chapter 4, where Jenny Corbett looks at the positive and negative aspects of the medical model. After this, a huge range of therapeutic approaches is considered in Chapter 5. These therapies have roots in medicine and psychology (not always happy bedfellows) and also link with some of the techniques, though not necessarily the philosophies, of occupational therapy and physiotherapy which are described in Chapter 7. Speech therapy, discussed by Jannet Wright in Chapter 6, is always a special case. Parents, as has been shown (Sandow, Stafford and Stafford, 1987) regard them more positively than any other professionals. They have a status which unfortunately is belied by career structure and salary.

4

It's his Condition, Mother: The Medical Model

Jenny Corbett

Introduction

What, you might ask, is the medical model? Does it vary as much as individual doctors do from tyranny to compliance? Doctors are accustomed to thinking sequentially about patients' 'problems'; they interrogate, examine, investigate, diagnose, treat and prognosticate with the potential for error at every step. On occasions they may appear preoccupied with the disability rather than the patient – orthopaedic surgeons at one time were suspected of looking more closely at the feet than the face, and many doctors speak too little to the child patient.

Hostility to the medical model, with its emphasis on the child's deficits rather than the limitations of suitable provision, has strengthened over recent years. I have long felt an ambivalence towards this challenge to the power of medical supremacy. Having grown up in a medical household where the treatment of disabled, sick and dying children was a not uncommon preoccupation, I found it difficult to perceive doctors as the oppressors of disabled people and as unsympathetic towards parents. With a paediatrician as a father, I saw the tensions, concern and uncertainty which struggling with difficult daily decisions presented him. To me, there was no sense of an authority who knew what was best but of a committed professional constantly having to cope with situations from which he was never emotionally detached. I suppose I was observing a consultant 'off-stage'. At home he could display that anxiety and distress which at work would have been considered inappropriate. Having visited hospital wards with him, I was aware that there he was 'centre-stage' with a chorus of nurses to support him. In such a position, he had to appear calm, efficient and decisive.

I have become increasingly aware that the medical model, with its patriarchal power structure, is damaging to both the recipients and the protagonists. It is dangerous for anyone to be treated as a deity. Doctors still may command that status, despite the erosion of their conditions of work and the chaos of health service changes. Yet they are as vulnerable as the rest of us and equally subject to external forces. When I reflected upon my father's career, which began with the birth of the National Health Service to which he was dedicated, I recorded the numerous factors which influenced medical practice and changed attitudes(Corbett, 1990). In this chapter I shall develop some of the themes I introduced in that appraisal of historical developments and set the issues into a current context.

I shall begin by examining the moral role and power of doctors and the extent to which this has changed. The significance given to diagnosis will be discussed in relation to intervention and its consequences. With reference to children with Down's syndrome, the dangers of setting a pessimistic prognosis will be examined. Exploring the position of doctors in a market culture, I shall ask, 'Who is the client?', as the Children Act 1989 places the child's needs as paramount. Perennial factors of economic depression, poverty and global pollution which cause disability and disease will be discussed in relation to the responsibility of doctors to engage in preventive measures. My approach is to try and understand how attitudes developed, changed and continue to be challenged.

A moral and patriarchal role

Whilst the medical profession has for many years been composed of a substantial proportion of women, it has developed from a patriarchal model which has informed its practice. Nowhere is this more evident than in the eugenics movement which selected grades of human beings, according to their perceived intellectual capacities. This development became well established as a significant and respectable research area, supported and sustained by powerful elements of the medical hierarchy. At its period of greatest influence in the early years of this century, eugenics fuelled racism, sexism and hostility against people with any form of disability. Even before Hitler was to employ this medical approach as his rationale for genocide, doctors were using eugenics to support their own prejudices.

As an example of applied eugenics in its heyday, two medical men link the deficits of 'idiots, imbeciles, morons and backward children' (Popenoe and Hill Johnson, 1920, p. 188) for whom they were designing colonies on barren land where they can be 'waste humanity taking waste land' (p. 189) with provision for 'women's special needs' (p. 378). They saw the 'spread of feminism' as a special need and expressed relief that these new women were not propagating themselves: 'Under the new regime a large proportion of such women do not marry, and accordingly have few if any children to inherit their defects' (p. 379).

From our current perspectives, we can marvel that such views were not only treated seriously but accorded high status in a medical text. The implication is that anyone who is a nuisance or who disturbs the status quo is evidently defective. It is important to examine such outrageous ideas which were once given credence as it enables us to understand how a mind-set can be legitimated and is only changed by active resistance. There were clear disadvantages for men in allowing women to become more independent and evident advantages in segregating less productive members of the community. If we recognize that we now feel indignant about such attitudes, we also need to reflect that people in years to come may feel similarly outraged that we permitted segregated educational provision to persist for so long and that a poor medical prognosis could mean an impoverished quality of life because of low expectations.

The issue of a child being born with a disability has become a contentious area for debate. The traditional medical approach is embodied in the Report of the Departmental Committee on Sterilization, produced by the Eugenics Society in 1934. The tone of the report is that it is taken for granted that disabled children are seen as a burden to themselves and society. The social judgements are significantly biased:

> We believe that few parents with any sense of responsibility who had had a defective child would not wish to examine the possibility that they were the victims of a hereditary weakness; and we feel strongly that they are entitled, if they wish it, to the protection of sterilization. We attach special importance to this recommendation because of its value in relation to the social problem group. There is abundant evidence that this group contributes much more than its numerical proportion to the total volume of defect, and an equal or even larger proportion of children of lower intelligence. This is not surprising, since the economic inefficiency of the defective tends to depress him to the lowest economic level. Defectives drift to the slums. Like marries like, and not only is the incidence of defect greater in this group, but the proportion of carriers is correspondingly greater.
>
> (Eugenics Society, 1934, pp. 41–2)

In statements such as this, the overt prejudice, hostility and élitism of the medical profession is frighteningly conveyed.

Morris (1991), a disabled feminist, discussed the topic of eugenics with particular reference to the Nazis and their policy of compulsory sterilization and euthanasia. Whilst she selected the most extreme and terrible use of the eugenics propaganda, it is vital to understand that this way of perceiving people was an acceptable part of the medical establishment for long after the Second World War. As Morris reflects,

> The arguments about whether disabled people's lives are worth living, and whether the medical profession should enable us to be 'released from misery' are as threatening today as they were in the Germany of the 1930s and early 1940s. In such a context, we must insist that our lives have value. We need to question fundamentally the assumption that to be disabled, to be different, means that life is not worth living.
>
> (Morris, 1991, p. 58)

Her discussion includes the current ethical challenges relating to embryo manipulation, in which she introduced the concept of the rights of a disabled foetus to have life.

It is interesting that Warnock (1992b), who chaired the influential Committee on Special Educational Needs, has also become deeply involved in this particular debate. Her response to the issue of 'aborting defective embryos' and to what she refers to as 'the handicapped lobby' (which presumably includes Morris) is to suggest that

> Of course if someone has been born, to say, 'It would have been better if, instead of you, someone else had been born', is harsh. But I do not think that this has anything to do with the wish that parents may have before anyone at all is born, that they may have a healthy rather than a fatally handicapped child. For when the healthy child is born there is no other child. The other potentially handicapped child never did come into existence. To choose this situation is not a reproach to any existing person at all. For the healthy child who is born is in no way identical with the handicapped child who might have been born (just as I am in no way identical with the hypothetical boy who was not born in my stead). So I cannot believe that aiming for healthy children by embryonic intervention is a reproach to any existing person. The preference is for existing healthy children over non-existent defective children.
>
> (Warnock, 1992b, p. 1048)

Hers is a philosophical argument founded on a specific approach to logical reasoning.

One of the key factors which emerges in these diverse views is that subjectivity determines perceptions of medical ethics. According to different ethical approaches, the birth of a disabled baby can be seen variously: as a social burden (Popenoe and Hill Johnson, 1920); as a celebration of the value of difference (Morris, 1991); with acceptance but a preference for healthy children (Warnock, 1992b). This subjectivity continues to be an influence on medical diagnosis, which tends to be presented as a clinical, scientific and accurate process.

Diagnosis and intervention

Johnston and Magrab (1976, p. 131) provide an explanation of why diagnosis has gained such importance in medical practice: 'Historically, early physicians treated all ailments similarly because of a failure to understand their underlying causes.'

Diagnosis is a process of understanding. As Solity (1992) notes, in relation to children having psychiatric problems, diagnosis has historically been developed in a neutral setting whereas it is now more likely that home and school environments and interactions will be explored. The child is no longer diagnosed at any stage without reference to the family.

When a baby or young child is diagnosed by the physician as having a disability, the complex and often stressful relationship between parents and professionals begins. There is great importance given to bonding straight after birth as a means of avoiding the rejection of a handicapped child by its disappointed parents. Paediatricians have to offer what they consider to be an honest diagnosis but the conveyer of 'bad news' is always in a difficult position. They may go to considerable lengths to help parents become receptive to the diagnosis, through a series of preliminary stages.

Health professionals continue to perceive the need for parents to heal the grief and work through a process of bereavement for the healthy child they did not have. Stewart and Pollack (1991), for example, suggest that:

> Adjustment to having a handicapped child is very complex and requires a family-integrated approach rather than one that is strictly child-centred. Having a handicapped child is a major crisis which creates conflict in its own right, and reactivates previous unresolved issues. It can be seen that there are similarities with bereavement through loss.
>
> (Stewart and Pollack 1991 p.248)

Whilst it is evident that such a life event requires a period of adjustment, as does the birth of any new baby, the extent to which it may be seen as a tragedy is socially constructed. What parents do seek from health professionals is a helpful approach. Sloper and Turner (1992) asked families of children with severe physical disability what they thought were the most important aspects of a helpful professional. They noted that:

> The majority (73%) mentioned a combination of approachability, openness and honesty, giving information and listening to parents. Other aspects mentioned were sensitivity and empathy (19%); treating

both the parent and the child as individuals and acknowledging the parents' role (16%); expert knowledge (14%); and giving practical help (12%).

(Sloper and Turner, 1992, p.270)

In order to provide such help, doctors are unable to remain detached. Parents may reject their disabled baby and the doctor might struggle to persuade them to reconsider their feelings, in the best interests of the child. Being honest and sensitive involves risk. The emotions of both parents and doctors are exposed in this process and the need for careful negotiation may become evident.

Intervention to prevent disease and disability includes economic as well as ethical considerations. In his analysis of the benefits of medical developments to prevent children being born with severe deafness and blindness resulting from rubella embryopathy in the first trimester of pregnancy, Corbett (1981) records the significant effects of mass immunization of schoolgirls. There are several aspects to the benefits of such intervention: the massive economic burden of providing services for multiply disabled children; women who have been immunized no longer fearing the possibility of passing on so severe a disability to their unborn baby; and, not least, the suffering experienced by many children with such disabilities. Whatever the arguments for celebrating the richness and diversity of difference, if certain disabilities involve significant experiences of physical suffering, this cannot be ignored. The 'quality of life' debate has worried doctors in relation to those young people they struggled to keep alive and then had to support through many successive operations and setbacks. Young people with spina bifida, for example, have gained a much improved chance of living but can experience considerable pain and suffering in their treatment and complications. Doctors may wish to ask, if termination of pregnancy for Down's syndrome is acceptable, should we strive to remedy major malformations (for example, heart and bowel obstructions) in the newborn baby with Down's syndrome? Parents may sometimes not wish for high technology to intervene and save the life of their newborn baby but feel overtaken by medical skills. If parents want their baby to be allowed to die, should doctors comply?

If we consider how improved medical knowledge has now almost eliminated childhood polio and deafness and blindness caused by rubella, is this not a positive advance? Is it not good to strive to prevent the occurrence of disabling conditions? From a medical practitioner's perspective, such a rhetorical question may appear nonsensical, as the evident value of this seems unequivocal. Yet there are other ways of seeing. Mason (1986, 1992) celebrates her role as a disabled mother of a disabled child. Rather than perceiving her daughter's birth as a tragedy, she saw it as a way in which she came to love and accept herself through loving her child and wanting the best for her. Her attitude is assertive and strong. Such an approach represents a challenge for the medical community in extending the boundaries of what constitutes acceptable normality (Corbett and Barton, 1992). If a parent does not see the disability as a burden, this alters the balance of power and redefines the role of professional services. Instead of 'It's his/her condition, mother' from the doctor, there is 'This is what we need' from the parents, accepting the child and demanding a right to services.

Relationships and prognosis

An indicator of the degree to which a patriarchal model was embedded in the medical tradition is the way in which nurses were socialized into deferential service roles:

> In health care, physicians have done the curing, using intellectual, scientific skills, while nurses have done the caring, using their 'natural female' attributes. Curing has been valued and recompensed; caring has not . . . . Despite growing resentment over the doctor – nurse game, nurses may have difficulty abandoning traditional rituals like making chart rounds, because to do so might mean conflict and the work of developing whole new ways of relating with physicians.
>
> (Muff, 1988, pp. 208–9)

Developing new relationships, whether between nurses and doctors or patients, parents and doctors, can involve conflict and stress. Maseide (1991, p. 552) suggests that medical power is maintained through the physicians' inclusion in a system of specific knowledge and skills, such that 'Physicians cannot, without serious consequences, decide to break the frame of their professional game. As integrated in institutionalised forms of knowledge and reasoning, they can only choose between more or less necessary forms of domination.' If a dominant power structure is acknowledged, then recent strategies to ease relationships can be seen as a way of making a necessary differential less marked.

It is clear that current medical practice is working towards placing more value on parental perspectives. Often parents seek help early and are not listened to but Herbert (1988) suggests that by the time some parents seek help from health professionals they may already have become demoralized and defeated. He sees it as the role of the professional adviser to give them back their dignity in the way in which they are listened to and seen as 'expert' on their own children. It is in the physician's interests to work closely with parents for

> Successful negotiation of therapeutic involvement is the professionals'
> task. A failure on the part of professionals to engage parents in therapy
> will not only lead to a lack of developmental progress, but also to a
> deterioration in longer-term function as the child continues to use
> maladaptive postures and movement patterns.
>
> (Cogher, Savage and Smith, 1992, p. 43)

The above reference was in relation to children with cerebral palsy, for whom regular physiotherapy and care in seating and feeding is fundamental to well-being and comfort. The authors recognize that mutual respect between doctors, therapists and parents is essential and that parents' views and expectations need to be understood. What doctors no longer seek is to be seen by parents as experts who take over all responsibility for the child.

Bax (1990) gives an illustration of what can happen between parents and professionals when the doctor's authority is treated with reverence. He was examining the development of young disabled adults after they had left school. He reflected that

> Most of the group with epilepsy were having anti-epileptic drugs, but in
> our view most of these drugs could have been stopped for the entire group
> without it making any difference to their epilepsy because the medication
> was so badly prescribed. I asked one mother when the medication had
> been prescribed and she said when her son had left Queen Mary's,
> Carshalton at the age of six. I thought for a moment and then I said, 'but
> he's 22 now.' She replied that the GP has increased the dose as her son has
> grown. The notion of blood levels and regular assessment of the
> treatment was not being considered. When I had been with the mother
> for an hour or so, she told me that sometimes she did not go to the surgery
> to pick up the prescription straight away, so her son was sometimes
> without his medication for a week or two; and this did not make any
> difference to the amount of fits he had. The curious factor was that she
> still had a guilt feeling that she should give the medication. How patients
> trust doctors – why go on giving a drug which does not work?
>
> (Bax, 1990, p. 66)

Bax's question gains even more force when asked of traditional medical prognosis. If a doctor tell parents that they should not expect much from their child with disabilities or learning difficulties, does this then mean that the family becomes locked into a self-fulfilling prophesy?

Perhaps nowhere has the danger of a poor prognosis been more powerfully demonstrated than in relation to children born with Down's syndrome. Physicians used to associate what they termed' Mongolian idiots' with racial degeneracy (Down, 1866). In his thorough study of the history of prognosis and treatment of people with Down's syndrome, Booth (1987) illustrates the ill-founded judgements and prejudices which doctors displayed. He concludes by saying that

> As a group, people with Down's syndrome are relatively incompetent at various tasks when compared with the population as a whole. But, the extent to which their physiognomy, or physical impairment or incompetence is a handicap depends on the way they are treated, the attitudes shown towards them, the provision made for them and the opportunities they are permitted.
>
> (Booth, 1987, p. 22)

Significant shifts in attitudes have led to enhanced choices and improved social developments (e.g. Atkinson and Williams, 1990; Sutcliffe, 1990, 1992). Children with Down's syndrome are now being integrated into mainstream schools, as parental expectations have increased. This is also a reflection of the market culture in which parents have a citizen's right to choice. However, such a right may not always work in favour of the child.

The market culture: who is the client?
Some parents choose to have cosmetic surgery performed on their child in a process which can alter those facial features which distinguish the child as having Down's syndrome. Other parents view this with considerable disquiet and decline to have it done to their own child. One parent reflected:

> If he was struggling with talking, say, I would have it done, but I must admit apart from that I can't see any reason – I would certainly leave his facial features the way they were. I can't see why that would be beneficial, to make him look normal. Maybe parents think other people will have a better attitude to them – they want their child to look as normal as possible. But they're not normal. They're cheating their child, by making them be more acceptable to society, I suppose, as a whole. To me, I must admit, they're changing their child, they're overruling the child to get this done . . . As far as surgeons are concerned, it's just a job to them, and it keeps them in a job. I just wonder what they do think, when a couple comes along. Their attitude is, 'This is a job. If that's what the parents want.' To me they should have a moral attitude . . . I don't want to judge professionals, but to me there's some things should be done and some things shouldn't be done.
>
> (parent quoted in Goodey, 1991, pp. 10–11)

This comment encapsulates the contradictions within a market model of healthcare. The parents have a right to ask for surgery which their child may neither consent to nor desire. Parents may simply want the child to look more socially acceptable, treating the human being like a consumable item. Should children's well-being become an element of the market-place?

In his critical response to conductive education, an intensive therapy for children with physical disabilities like cerebral palsy, Oliver (1989) implies that forcing children to walk when it may be a terrible strain for them can be seen as a form of cruelty. When can treatments, which may involve the whole family facing upheaval and emotional pressure and place considerable responsibility on the child to progress, become torture? Is there a thin dividing-line between encouraging high parental expectations and placing the child concerned at risk?

Children's rights

The Children Act 1989 has introduced a concept of 'children in need' which broadly includes both those at risk from neglect and abuse and those with disabilities. As Russell (1991) says,

> Many of the children defined as being 'in need' under the Children Act will also have special educational needs under the 1981 Education Act. Possibly because of this fact the new arrangements offer a unique (and perhaps definitive) opportunity to develop genuinely interdisciplinary ways of planning and implementing services for individual children which draw upon the expertise of health and education, as well as social services, and which reflect the wishes and concerns of children and parents.
>
> (Russell, 1991, p. 115)

The Children Act has placed the child's perceptions of his or her own needs as central, in a way that challenges the traditional model of expert authority and parental power. Children are now able to 'divorce' their parents if they feel this is in their best interests. Such a development is still in the early throes of legal and ethical dilemmas but has profound implications for the future. It shifts the balance of power in a way which gives status, credibility and strength to children, who traditionally have been a powerless and oppressed social group.

Recent compilations of the various forms which child abuse can take (e.g. Meadow, 1991) indicate that parents can burn, scald, poison or suffocate their children and can emotionally abuse them to the extent that they fail to grow naturally, as well as beating or sexually abusing them. The paediatrician's responsibility is often for babies or very young children who are not yet able to communicate their fears, other than by outwardly visible signs. Assessing mental cruelty may be particularly difficult to prove. In her evaluation of legal proceedings, Mitchels (1991), a solicitor working to protect children under the powers of the Children Act 1989, recognizes that 'the needs and welfare of the child are balanced against the rights of parents and the legal requirements of the courts' (p. 45). This involves close collaboration between doctors, lawyers and social workers.

Already, some excellent examples are emerging of effective multiprofessional teamwork on behalf of children. In a recent instance (Wiseman *et al.*, 1992), psychiatrists, psychologists, social workers, lawyers, police and paediatricians worked together to assess the reliability of videotaped interviews with children suspected of being sexually abused. The increased emphasis given to the experience of sexual abuse among sometimes very young children is an indicator of doctors' heightened awareness of potential risk. What young children say has happened to them is listened to and taken seriously by adults who are in a position to help. This, in itself, is significant. It is not that child sexual abuse is a new phenomenon but that adults in positions of authority are treating children's views as having credibility. In my examination of my father's career, I speculated as to why, in the 1970s, he had been so acutely alert to the 'battered baby syndrome' and yet almost unaware of instances of child sexual abuse. He was of the generation of paediatricians who were taught how to diagnose fractures which could only be explained by deliberate physical abuse but were not taught how to diagnose children who had been sexually abused.

This example demonstrates that it is essential for doctors to update their knowledge constantly in order to ensure the best possible level of care. Jones (1992) illustrates that in-service education is an integral component of any effective primary healthcare team. However, in order for doctors to work at peak efficiency, they need to feel valued and confident. Conditions of service in recent years have eroded their status and created uncomfortable hierarchies in which medical practitioners can feel bullied by 'macho' management techniques (Simpson and Smith, 1992). Not only are doctors feeling disempowered by management structures, they are also increasingly pressurized into unrealistic time constraints in busy clinics where parental concerns cannot be fully addressed. This can damage the quality of listening on both sides:

> Professionals may choose not to hear what has been said for a variety of reasons, such as protecting the family or because of their own discomfort at being unable to help and address the families' concerns directly. Similarly, parents may not hear what has been said, due to their own mental blocks or simply because they are being barraged with too much technical information.
>
> (Stallard and Lenton, 1992, p. 202)

The effects of stress, at all levels, cannot be underestimated as a cause of misunderstanding, frustration and disharmony.

The politics of medicine
Many external factors determine the quality of healthcare. Among the current issues for debate are the following: the impact of entrepreneurial medical intervention from the West upon healthcare in Russia (Delamothe, 1992); the deteriorating services in the capital as just one aspect of London's malaise (Smith, 1992a); the growth of unemployment and homelessness increasing ill health (Delamothe, 1992); pressure on doctors in certain parts of the world to participate in torture (Vanes, 1992); the protests of young black people with sickle-cell anaemia who are accused of being drug addicts if they ask for morphine when in crisis (BBC 1, 1992); toxic dumping, filthy industries and nuclear testing being the cause of disease in Russia (Hearst, 1992). These are current topics of news interest. They indicate the contribution made by war, recession, prejudice and power struggles to the creation of disease and disability.

Booth (1992) notes that approximately 660,000 children have AIDS world-wide, mostly in parts of sub-Saharan Africa, the Caribbean and South America. Russell (1992), in recording examples of HIV-infected children in the UK, shows that schools have to learn how to support staff and students. She gives the example of thirteen-year-old Peter, who was frightened that his brother might have AIDS through drug abuse:

> The school arranged a special 'whole school programme' about AIDS and HIV, with the local authority AIDS coordinator and a consultant from the local Haemophilia Unit (both well known in the community) to answer questions. The presentation focused on the importance of seeing people and families affected by HIV as ordinary people.
>
> (Russell, 1992, p. 274)

Orton (1989) emphasizes that children with many complex medical conditions, who used to be placed in the care of special schools in the recent past, are now being integrated successfully. Teachers are taught about asthma, anorexia nervosa, coeliac disease, cystic fibrosis, diabetes, epilepsy, haemophilia, leukaemia, or whatever the disease or disability may be of the children in their care. Sick, or even dying, children should continue to be part of the school community. In the school where my husband teachers, for example, a pupil aged twelve recently died from leukaemia. He attended school and participated in as many activities as possible up to a few days before he died. If the doctor helps a family to cope with a dying child, whether in school or in a hospice, this offers a positive support of shared responsibility.

Conclusion

The paternalism of past medical practice in which doctors saw 'the poor' as passive dependents who were hopelessly inadequate (e.g. Hannington, 1937) is now perceived as inappropriate. Collaboration and good communication, with ideas presented patiently, with honesty and openness, is being promoted in healthcare (Holinger, 1989; Urbano, 1992; Murphy, 1992). Yet, Sloper and Turner (1992) imply that improvements are still required in information services to families, available resources and co-ordination of services if parents of children with disabilities are to have real choice of services.

Two significant forces for change challenge the medical model in quite distinct directions. The Disability Movement (Barnes, 1992) wants to give disabled people power over their own bodies, to direct their own healthcare needs without being made to feel burdens by the medical profession and related caring organizations. The Children Act 1989 supports the rights of children to speak up for their own needs, which may create tensions and disunity with their parents. It is no longer an issue simply of parents relating to professionals but of disabled people and children asserting their rights.

Acknowledgement

I am very grateful to my father, Richard Pugh, for his invaluable comments on earlier drafts of this chapter.

For the reader

Why did a medical model become so significant in special education and how has it been challenged? In what main ways are disabled activists changing the medical model into a social model of disability? If the child is the client of a paediatrician, what consequences can this have for parents?

5

It's not about Happy Endings: Individual and Family Therapies

Sarah Sandow and Anne Stokes

Psychology is about exploring human behaviour and human consciousness. Because psychology has roots in philosophy, science and medicine, the various roles of those who examine human experience become confused and the lay observer sometimes finds it hard to differentiate the educational psychologist who deals mainly with immediate presenting problems of learning and behaviour, from the medically qualified psychiatrist, who may be concerned with underlying tensions and difficulties. However, an educational or clinical psychologist may wish to operate within a psychodynamic framework, and a psychiatrist may prefer a behavioural approach. To add to the confusion, others, such as psychiatric social workers, therapists or counsellors, may adopt one or more of a range of approaches when dealing with emotional issues with individuals or within the context of the family.

This chapter will give a brief, necessarily limited, overview of a range of therapeutic approaches, and will discuss some of the issues and problems that arise from them. Methods commonly used with individuals will be described first, followed by an account of some ways of working with families. Thirdly, creative therapies will be considered and the chapter will end with a short discussion on the implications of therapeutic approaches for teachers.

For the purpose of this chapter, the generic term 'therapists' will be used for simplicity, whether referring to counsellors or psychotherapists. There is difficulty in making a clear distinction between these two, though a rough and ready guide might be that counselling is often for shorter periods than psychotherapy, and that in addition psychotherapists may work with clients at a deeper level. However, whenever the two come together this difference will be disputed. Dryden and Feltham (1992) take the view that there is no essential difference between them as both 'aim to alleviate human suffering, solve problems and help people to live more satisfying lives'.

Children with special educational needs, whether they have learning difficulties or exhibit behaviour problems or both, are inevitably a source of anxiety to their families, and sometimes to themselves. Many parents and many young people cope with these anxieties as well as others cope with the difficulties in their own lives, and we would not wish to argue that all families or individuals whose lives are touched by disability need the support of a therapist. However, some do need help. The shock of discovering that a long-awaited child has been born with severe learning difficulties and physical handicaps; the discovery of an incipient degenerative condition; a situation where parents (or grandparents) blame each other for the problem; an ambitious family having to adjust to different expectations for a child's future; all these may lead a parent to seek counselling. A child or young person may need help in coping with problems of impetuousness, of failing to live up to expectations, or the frustration of constant failure.

In any case, the person (or 'client') who enters a therapeutic relationship will be expected to work on their own problem with the support of the therapist. A difficulty which seems to be built into the process is the external expectation that once a client has worked on the presenting issue, be it a relationship, a behavioural problem or a problem of self-esteem, then she or he will live, as in the fairy tales, happily ever after. However, the therapist has no magic wand, and real life is not often like that. Lake and Acheson (1988) suggest that the objective of 'the therapy movement', which embraces counselling, psychotherapy and, to some extent, psychoanalysis, is to enable clients to become psychologically or emotionally fitter, which will in turn help them to get more from life, be more fulfilled and possibly happier.

In practical terms, the therapist will be a trained professional, meeting for about an hour with the client(s), who may be hesitant about being there, particularly at first or if they have been referred rather than seeking the help themselves. They will be encouraged to do most of the talking, with the therapist listening and observing for most of the time and there may be longer periods of silence than in normal conversations to allow the client to reflect. Often the client will expect the therapist to tell them what to do and will be looking for 'expert' answers. The role of the therapist is generally that of being alongside the clients in their journey, helping them to find their own answers from within, rather than having solutions imposed on them from the outside. Although in time most clients come to understand and value this process and recognize that they are the experts on themselves, some initially view it as a time-consuming and frustrating experience. Others working with the client, such as parents, teachers and social workers, may be helped, and of help, by recognizing that this is part of the process.

While individual therapy may be right for some children, others are offered it not because that is the best road for them but because it is the only help available or because the family does not wish to take part in joint therapy. Before looking at family therapy, it will be useful therefore to outline the main approaches to individual therapy. These may also be used to a greater or lesser degree in the joint process. There are vast numbers of different therapies, but as a working guide they may be divided into three main schools of thought known as psychodynamic, humanistic and cognitive–behavioural. While these are outlined below as if separate and unconnected approaches, it should be noted that therapists may also adopt an integrated way of working, whereby they blend together concepts and techniques from a number of therapies into their own specific approach. Others may be rooted in one approach but may also use insights and experiences from others where they feel that this would be of use to a particular client or a particular issue.

Psychodynamic therapies

Psychodynamic theory and practice have evolved from Freud's work, and during the development from early psychoanalysis there have been many models, methods and philosophies which are very close to his evolving theories and also others which now seem quite unrelated to it. It would be confusing in a short account to give a detailed description of the different theoretical positions, but a psychodynamic therapist will be rooted in developmental psychology of, for example, Sigmund, Freud, Anna Freud, Klein, Jung or Erikson.

'Psyche' is used to refer to the three aspects of the person – intellectual, emotional and spiritual (in the broadest sense) – and not just the first as is sometimes thought. 'Dynamic' refers to the way in which the psyche is seen as active, with the activity taking place in relationship to people and objects outside the 'self', and also importantly in relationships within the self. The idea of having a number of selves may seem absurd or far-fetched until we recall phrases in common usage such as 'I don't feel like myself today', 'I felt really angry with myself' or 'part of me feels this and part of me feels that'. The parts of the self are known by various terms including Freud's, id, ego and super-ego, and the Parent, Adult, Child of transactional analysis.

These 'selves' may be developed over the period of our childhood, through adolescence and into adulthood, with the experiences in the early years being seen as particularly crucial. For this reason, a psychodynamic therapist would pay particular attention to the experiences and emotions in a client's past. Both are relevant as it is not merely what has happened, but also the way a child has internalized it, that affects the present. If 'I' am angry with 'myself' it may well have something to do with the way in which my parents or significant adults were cross with me or I perceived them to be. This may well have become part of the punitive self: the super-ego or the conscience. While these early internalized perceptions are modified over the years in light of different experiences, they appear to be rarely lost altogether. In time of stress or crises, older children and adults may find themselves back in those early ways of perceiving and acting; technically this is known as 'regression'.

There are a number of other specific technical terms which are associated with the psychodynamic approach. These are sometimes used more loosely and often incorrectly in everyday conversation. It may be helpful to look at just two of these. The unconscious is (obviously) material that is not conscious and is hidden in some way from the client. Even when a person can recall the event, the feelings which go with it may not be accessible or remembered. There is a difference between the unconscious and the preconscious from which it is much easier to recall memories. Feelings and complete episodes may be kept unconscious because they are seen to be too painful or dangerous to acknowledge. Part of the process of therapy will be to look at these in a safe and supportive relationship at the client's pace. If it seems difficult to believe that we can so effectively hide things from ourselves, we need only to think about accounts of childhood abuse recalled by adults who had buried the memories so effectively that they had 'forgotten' that it had taken place.

The therapeutic relationship is seen as important in most approaches, but there is a particular aspect of the relationship which is of importance in psychodynamic therapy – that of transference. This is seen as happening in every human relationship to a greater or lesser degree, and while therapists from other schools may acknowledge its existence, it is primarily in this approach that therapists will work with it. Jacobs (1988) defines it thus:

> Briefly, transference is the repetition by the client of old child-like patterns of relating to significant people, such as parents, but now seen in relationship to the counsellor . . . [who] becomes, for the client, a transference figure with whom the client has the opportunity to relive the . . . parent-child relationship.
>
> (Jacobs, 1988)

Transference can be positive or negative, depending on the original relationship. Where it is negative it may prove difficult for the client to trust or accept the therapist, but it may give useful insights to be worked on, which in turn enable the client's progress.

If transference seems fanciful, or to belong only in the realm of therapy, teachers may recall the occasions when they are called 'mum' or 'dad' by their students. In social situations, when we make snap decisions, sometimes without even talking to a person, that we like or do not like them, it may be worth asking ourselves if there is anything about them – physically or in mannerism or in speech – that reminds us of someone from our past.

For a readable and in-depth account of the psychodynamic approach, the reader is referred to *Psychodynamic Counselling in Action* by Michael Jacobs (1988). Here the author uses two of Dickens's characters to show how he would have worked with them if they had presented themselves to him in therapy.

In summary, as Lake and Acheson (1988) suggest, psychodynamic therapy has some similarities with taking day-trips back into childhood. When the client returns from there, she may apply the conclusions drawn in looking around, to the present.

Some have attempted to undertake psychoanalysis and psychotherapies with people who have learning difficulties. However, there are two problems with this. First, psychotherapies are essentially language based. The more severe the learning difficulty, the greater the probability that expressive language and comprehension will be affected (see Chapter 6, p. 82) It is therefore less likely that the individual will be able to participate fully in a therapeutic experience which requires emotional expression through language. Secondly, there is an increased probability that the therapist will invest the verbal and even the non-verbal behaviour of the client with a sophistication which may not be justified. Sinason has written extensively about her experience in treating handicapped children and adults. She separates cognitive from affective states and skills, and argues that 'there seems no clear one-to-one relationship between cognitive and emotional understanding'. She describes a fourteen-year-old severely handicapped boy who could not recognize the picture of a knife in a word recognition test. 'The quality of this non-recognition was not to do with consciously withholding knowledge but a quite powerful unconscious blocking of a subconscious memory. In therapy . . . the week before he had described cutting his wrist with a knife' (Stokes and Sinason, 1992, p. 51). But could the boy not simply have failed to associate the picture of a knife with the object itself? Or even more simply, have forgotten the previous conversation?

Many developmental psychologists would question the independence of cognition and affect. Conceptually, both are dependent upon a degree of linguistic competence. Hinchcliffe and Roberts (1987, and see Chapter 9) have explored the great difficulties of teaching the meaning of emotional-state words to young people with severe learning difficulties. This is not to say that the experience of complex emotion is beyond the individual, but the recognition and labelling of affective states is a different matter. This is recognized by McGuire and Tynan who indicate that 'it has often been beneficial in our work to teach the meanings of particular feelings and emotions using pictures and modelling before proceeding with counselling of emotive issues' (McGuire and Tynan, 1992, p. 241).

It seems reasonable to assume that a psychotherapeutic intervention which is dependent on the retention of thoughts and experiences, and requires the client to continue to 'work' on the process of self-analysis and adjustment will have limited application to a severely handicapped individual. However, there is no clear boundary between severe learning difficulties and less serious handicaps. The judgement of how relevant a 'talking therapy' may be is a fine one; but it must be important to be parsimonious in interpretation. Judd (1990) writes of the psychotherapy of Sharon, a seventeen-year-old girl with spina bifida and hydrocephalus, with an IQ in the SLD (severe learning difficulties) range. The sensitive, moving description makes it clear that, over time, the girl developed a warm relationship with the therapist, in which she was supported in her cognitive and emotional development. Judd herself writes of her realization that the disabled 'can have scant conscious awareness that anything is lacking'. However, she also takes the view that 'we have an instinctive knowledge of wholeness' and that we 'can work towards acknowledging any deficits'. She has respect for the girl that might have been, but the Sharon that exists is viewed as not being 'truly alive', because she has not 'risked the enormous range of painful feelings about her own plight' (Judd, 1990)[1].

Wholeness is relative. Deficit must be in the eye of the beholder, as Judd acknowledges. Perhaps it is the beholder whose psychotherapeutic journey is described. Sharon evidently exhibits the 'cocktail party syndrome', the endless stream of words which give the impression of verbal facility greater than other abilities. It may be over-interpretive, however, to suggest that the 'indiscriminate desperate need to pour out her words without interruption . . . is a displacement on to concretized words of her infant self's needs for a vital flow of urine/faeces/verbal babble, which is felt to be under her control'.

Sharon is, like other clients, individuals or families, being invited to 'reframe' her experience. But is the new frame really that of the therapist? The implicit value judgement of the therapist can be dangerous: just as Sharon's self-concept may only be deviant in the observer's view, and this interpretation and intervention may be disabling. 'The structure of psychotherapy is such that no matter how kindly a person is, he or she is engaged in acts that are bound to diminish the dignity, autonomy and freedom of the person who comes for help' (Masson, 1990, p. 25).

Segal (1989) in her therapy with people with physical, intellectual and emotional disabilities using a Kleinian approach, has evolved a number of principles for counselling:

(1) Use of language should reflect the fact that people with disabilities are first and foremost people.
(2) A disability, chronic illness or handicap affects whole families and social networks, not just the individual.
(3) The meaning of the disability is as important as the disability itself.
(4) People with disabilities and handicaps should be offered counselling which is as near to 'normal' as possible.
(5) Confronting reality in a skilled way is an essential ingredient of counselling whatever the problem.

Counsellors as well as others can be caught by the assumption that illness, a distorted body, a difficulty in speaking or a slowness of intellectual grasp must all be accompanied by a lack of emotional strength.

It is suggested that it is the able-bodied counsellor rather than the client who may be afraid of confronting the difficulties, by avoiding or blocking opportunities to discuss expression of disquieting and painful beliefs, experiences and perceptions.

One of the issues arising in work with people with disabilities focuses on grieving for the loss of what might have been; this is also true for members of their family. In trying to make sense of the situation, it is often felt that it must somehow be someone's fault, so feelings of guilt may well need to be worked on, including those around the desire to wish the disability on to someone else. Because disability is seen in some senses as an affront to society and/or the medical world, there can be a desire to make things better. While this may be more obvious in parents' desires for their children, the likelihood of children with a learning difficulty also wanting to make their parents better – less unhappy, less tired, less stressed – should not be overlooked.

Often it is assumed that with the loss of an ability must come the loss of a role, and in family therapy this may be examined. Those with disability, and their families, have to cope with the anxieties and revulsion of those with whom they come into contact. Segal (1989, p. 337) reminds us that as in all counselling, when the client 'is complaining about the attitude of "society" or someone close to them, it can be useful to ask "and is there a part of you that agrees with them?"' While this may seem a hard thing to do it demonstrates two things. First the principle stated above, of counselling people as people first and foremost. Second, it demonstrates that therapy is not about making it all come right or working in a cosy, comforting manner.

Humanistic therapy

Humanistic psychology is centred in the 'here and now' rather than in the past, with the emphasis on current relationships. The influence of the past in shaping us is not discounted, but it is not seen as essential to understand the past, unless it is seen as preventing us from moving on.

Perhaps the best known example of this school is person-centred therapy. This began with the work of Carl Rogers who initially termed it non-directive from his philosophy that people are experts on themselves and do not need to be given interpretations or advice by experts on how to live. What they do need is time and space to be able to find their own solutions. As Rogers himself said, 'I know that I cannot teach anyone anything: I can only provide an environment in which they can learn' (Rogers, 1983). The therapist is seen as the person who helps to provide the relationship in which that can happen. His or her role is to listen to the client in a supportive and non-judgemental way, the notion of unconditional positive regard being seen as central to this approach. 'It is often by being allowed to express ourselves and "hear" ourselves, through another person listening to us, that we are able to find our solutions' (Burnard, 1992, p.21).

As stated above, the relationship between client and therapist is also important in the psychodynamic approach. The difference between the two is that in person-centred therapy the relationship is seen as being sufficient in itself to enable change to take place, as long as there are the three core conditions within it. The first of these is unconditional positive regard. This does not mean approval of everything a client may say or do but rather it 'requires a caring and a prizing of the client as a whole person' (Merry, 1988). It is an acceptance of the client as they are at that moment, and knowing that there is more to them than just that one facet. It enables the client to express disturbing and conflicting anxieties in safety.

For many professionals working with children, this concept can cause immense concern. They feel that they are being asked to condone all manner of antisocial (and anti-self) behaviour. That is not the case: what they are being asked to do is first accept the person. Parents surely have to learn to do this all the time, they still love and accept their child at a deep level, even while rejecting specific actions or behaviours.

The second core condition is congruence. This means that the therapist is present in the relationship in an honest and open way, and is aware of his or her own feelings in that relationship. These are not always expressed as it is the client's issues that are of concern, but if they impede the ability to listen to the client, it may well be better to express them in an appropriate way. It is partly through this expression that the client may be helped to build a real relationship with the therapist and learn through it to be truly accepting of self.

Empathy is the third core condition, which has a particular meaning in the therapeutic relationship. It is not sympathy which is made up of compassion, pity and usually the desire to make the other person feel better. Nor is it telling the other person that 'we know how she feels'. Even if we have experienced a similar happening, the birth of a child with disability, for example, we have not experienced the same thing. No two people will have exactly the same feelings or perceptions, and while sympathy is an essential part of our human nature, in therapy it is only by listening to the client telling her story, that we can truly understand what this event means to her. It is to this entering of the client's world that the term empathy refers. It is also listening not just to the words, but to the background tune – the half-expressed feelings. In being empathic, the therapist will constantly check that she has been accurate in understanding and will be guided by the responses which are received.

Two major criticisms are often levelled against person-centred therapy. The first is that it has no sense of structure; however, this is where 'non-directive' is muddled with lack of purpose. The process is not 'soft-and-warm-and-fuzzy', but in enabling clients to explore their world safely, the therapist does not shrink from challenging and confronting inconsistencies.

The second criticism, of relevance to those working with children with special needs, is that it is only useful to the very articulate or 'chattering middle classes'. Increasingly, there are therapists who work through the medium of the expressive arts using the person-centred approach. Natalie Rogers (Carl Rogers' daughter) has pioneered this work at the Person Centred Expressive Therapy Institute in California. Here art, pottery, music, dream work and movement, rather than words, are used to facilitate clients. This venture has led some to suggest that it is too directive, but Thorne (1992), amongst others, bears witness that 'the creation of facilitative conditions is essential to its success and that there is no sense in which clients are coerced into forms of expression which they have not willingly embraced'. An overview of creative therapy is given later in the chapter.

Rogers' book *Freedom to Learn for the Eighties* (1983) expands his philosophy and is of particular relevance to those in education. The last major school of thought may be divided into two subdivisions: behaviour and cognitive behavioural therapy.

Behaviour therapy
The most common therapy utilized with individuals with learning difficulties is simple behaviour therapy. This differs from the foregoing approaches because it emphasizes a change in behaviour, which may be accompanied by new insight, rather than a development of new insight which may be accompanied

by a change in behaviour. In behaviour therapy, the antecedents and the consequences of established behaviours are identified, and clients are taught how these may be altered in order to reshape the behaviour. New desired behaviours are rewarded, at first continuously, and then as the behaviours become established, with diminishing frequency. The method is often used where a specific maladaptive behaviour is involved. For example, a child gets into the habit of avoiding school. In the morning she lies in bed while her mother shouts at her to get up. There is a daily row which takes so long that she is late. When she gets to school she is so late that she is reprimanded, so she decides not to turn up at all. Changing the antecedents, (the row) and the consequences (the reprimand) enables a change in the girl's behaviour. At a time when accountability and cost-effectiveness are stressed, the fact that behaviour therapy can achieve clear results for difficult and distressing problems such as school refusal or enuresis makes it very attractive.

However, there can be dangers. We may consider the analogy of the headache: behaviour therapy is like the aspirin which removes the headache and enables normal functioning; however, the aspirin does not reach an underlying neurological condition, and may return in a more virulent form once the aspirin has worn off. In many cases the aspirin will suffice, but sometimes a more extensive investigation is indicated. (Perhaps the girl is avoiding school for some particular reason which is worth investigating?) Behaviour therapy has been extensively used with individuals who have severe learning difficulties and has been instrumental in eliminating painful and distressing behaviour like self-injury. Nevertheless, it has been suggested that, effective though it may be for dealing with some problems, 'this approach does not recognise adequately the humanity of the client being treated' (McGuire and Tynan, 1992). The degree to which an individual is able to participate in the decision-making inherent in a behavioural approach may be related to the degree of disability, and as the same authors remark, people with severe disabilities may have become 'highly suggestible and compliant'.

Cognitive behavioural therapy

In the first century AD, Epictetus stated that 'Men are disturbed not by things, but the view they take of them.' According to Trower, Casey and Dryden (1988), this could be seen as the central core of cognitive behavioural therapy. These views or interpretations of experiences are merely hypotheses, but the clients have come to see them as unchangeable facts. When they hold negative views about themselves, they will interpret these as facts, and therefore emotional upset will occur. It is the therapist's role therefore to help the client dispute these beliefs and change his behaviour in light of this new awareness. As in behaviour therapy, tasks will often be incorporated into the treatment process, in this case not solely to change the behaviour, but rather to dispute and demonstrate the dysfunctional thinking. It is hoped that by having a structured approach to doing this the client will be able to apply this in a generalized way in other areas of life.

For this reason amongst others, cognitive behavioural therapy (CBT) is often thought of as being a particularly suitable approach for brief therapy. Currently it is difficult to obtain long-term therapy through the NHS, so that when therapy is offered it is usually for a specific duration of between six and twelve sessions. A problem-focused approach may therefore be seen as being the most useful. In terms of the client group considered in this book, this may have serious implications since as Dryden and Feltham (1992, p. 6) state, 'brief counselling clients should be preferably functioning reasonably well . . .. They should be capable of formulating their problems reasonably succinctly.' While not all families or individuals with special needs fall outside these parameters, for many, perhaps because of earlier lack of support, there may be enormous difficulties in 'functioning reasonably well'.

It should not be read into the above that CBT is only used as a short-term therapy. As in the other major approaches, the long-term relationship is important, though here it is because the dysfunctional thinking about relation-ships in general may well be mirrored in the therapeutic relationship. In disputing the thinking by drawing on their own relationship, the confidence can be given to work on others outside.

CBT has been mistakenly linked to 'the power of positive thinking'. Trower *et al.* (1988) argue that it is in fact about realistic thinking. There are situations in a client's life where it would be dysfunctional to take a completely positive view, where this also would be a twisting of the truth. Therapy helps the client to understand that although the situation is very difficult, it does not have to be completely overwhelming. For example, when a child has a severe disability, it would be unethical to get the parents to move towards a view where they saw it as a totally positive experience. However, they might be encouraged to dispute their held view that they could not enjoy any relationship with the child, or that every part of their life was catastrophic. It is not an easy task for the therapist to show empathy towards clients, not disregard the magnitude of their issues, and at the same time enable them to look realistically at their beliefs. Such is the aim of CBT.

Family therapies
Focus on the family is not intended to replace a 'blame the child' model with a 'blame the family' one. During the 1940s and 1950s the work of Laing (1959)

with schizophrenics and of Kanner (1944) with autistic children led to the public view that therapists believed parents in particular were blameworthy in respect of their child's difficulties. In the context of the medical model discussed in Chapter 4, it is easy to see that this perception coloured attitudes towards intervention with families. The non-judgemental, more person-centred approach in family therapy, however, seems to initiate a process of change in attitudes, approaches and management on the part of the family without apportioning blame.

Every family, however made up of parent of parents, children, grandparents or others, is perceived as a system of interlocking relationships which may be positive and liberating or negative and inhibiting. Each member of the family has a perspective on the whole system, which governs their own pattern of initiating, or responding to, events. Where, within a family, one individual is identified as having an obvious problem, disability or handicap, this person may become the focus of family activity. Of course this is natural. Households and families need to look after their weaker members. Where therapists become involved, it may be because this focus has become distorted or the activities counterproductive.

Walrond-Skinner (1976) writes that the attributes of individuals or 'components' of a system can only be understood as functions of the total system. By a system is meant the complex network of relationships which structure an individual's existence. Thus, individual psychopathology is seen as having less explanatory power than the way in which the individual habitually initiates and responds to communications of different social groups. We can understand this if we think about the different way in which we behave in each of the different systems of which we are a part: home, work, friendship groups, and so on. It is very common, for example, for parents and teachers to have a very different perspective on the behaviour of a child, which leads one or the other to say 'He's perfectly all right with me' (a statement which, of itself, can lead to a breakdown in relations!).

Within a family system there will be patterns of dominance which are not necessarily immediately apparent to the members. We all know families (perhaps our own) where a parent, perhaps a father, believes himself to be in charge, but where in fact the power lies elsewhere. 'He makes the important decisions, like whether we should sign the Maastricht Treaty, and I make the unimportant ones, like whether we should go on holiday.' Sometimes power lies with one of the apparently junior members, like the child who throws tantrums in public places in order to get what she wants. A physically disabled child, generally indulged by everyone at home, was able to control totally her family's television-watching habits by merely 'pulling a pet lip' every time something not to her liking was switched on.

Within the system there will also be 'alliances': fathers and daughters, mothers and sons (or vice versa), parents and children, or any other possible permutation. These alliances may be positive, or they may sometimes be coercive or manipulative. 'Dad said I could', 'Nan gave me the money', 'I'm sure you don't want me to tell your father about this', 'Don't nag the child, she didn't mean it, did you?'

Where there is a serious problem in the family, these patterns of dominance and subservience, and these alliances can lead to what therapists term 'disordered interplay' between family members, which may be ultimately destructive and discomfiting. The individual who is presented to the therapist as the one with the problem may develop a behaviour disorder, such as tantrums, bedwetting or stealing, or she many withdraw altogether from the family, not speaking or interacting normally, or she may show serious symptoms of anxiety, such as insomnia, weeping or abnormal fears (Campion, 1985).

The task of the therapist is to help the family to redefine the problem and to focus their attention on the ways in which they may be maintaining a situation which they all find disagreeable. The emphasis may not be on changing the basic situation (in the case of a child with a disability this may not be possible anyway), but on finding new ways of coping, and on changing those attitudes and responses which prevent coping. The therapist will seek to understand the ways in which the family communicates, and see if there are ways in which the family members can relate differently, reconciling the needs of all. What does the family 'do with' the disability? Do they think about 'the disabled person' or 'the disability'? Does the family, or do some members of it, actually need the disability? If so, then change may be unwanted, even though it seems desirable. Stokes and Sinason describe the dilemma of parents with an adult handicapped child who:

> may not be able to give up their parental role. Sometimes, the only way they can stay bearing a parental function while other parents are slowly freed of it is to bond in a way that they did with much younger children. Without this, they would not be able to stay attached.
>
> (Stokes and Sinason, 1992, p. 49)

Thus we may understand why middle-aged women with Down's syndrome are sometimes to be seen wearing ankle socks and hair-ribbons and holding hands with their elderly parents.

The central process which the therapists seeks to initiate is called 'reframing'. This means 'the process whereby people come to think about and experience their situation differently' (Flaskas, 1992). In lay terms it may mean 'coming to terms with', 'adjusting to', 'learning to cope with' the problem, but as a family, rather than as one individual. It is also very much about actually seeing the issue differently so that it is no longer a problem. Thus with the middle-aged women with Down's syndrome, the parents might come to find a way of either staying attached without needing to see their daughter as a child, or dealing with the issues of separation.

The relative silence of the one-to-one therapies is usually replaced in family therapy by one of a number of other interventions such as direct questions, suggestions or hypotheses, or reflecting comment by the therapist (Owen, 1992). The therapist will note who talks, who listens, what kind of talking it is, and to whom it is addressed, what alliances are revealed, what pattern of dominance and subservience can be observed.

In *systemic* family therapy, as has been shown, the therapist will be concerned with the way established behaviour patterns serve the family's view of the world and itself within the world. In structural family therapy the emphasis will be on the way the transactions between family members serve to reinforce or threaten the structure of the family. This structure, which is essentially a pattern of expectations, is maintained by the predictable behaviours of the family members to one another. Some family structures can be too close, overinvolved and stifling, some too distant and unsupportive. Minuchin and Fishman (1981) emphasized the importance of establishing boundaries between family members.

Strategic family therapy focuses on a particular problem presented by one or more family members and attempts to restructure the family's response to that problem. Sometimes it appears that the habitual ways of solving the problem have had the opposite effect of maintaining it. For example, an adolescent autistic boy was fully toilet trained at school each day, but not at home. It was discovered that on his arrival at home each day, his mother immediately put him in a nappy, whereupon he defecated. Her strategy for avoiding accidents had the effect of (a) increasing his dependence upon a ritual and (b) preventing him from learning to use the toilet. Strategic therapy would have attempted in this case to change the mother's way of responding to the problem, by demonstrating to her that her actions were paradoxically supporting it (Campion, 1985).

There are a number of advantages of using family therapy. The most obvious has already been alluded to: the issues around special needs rarely rest solely in one person. Also clients can be better understood through seeing them interact within their families, and there can be practice in trying out new ways of relating to each other in the safety of the therapy room. It could also be argued on the grounds of cost. It is cheaper to see the family together, rather than in separate individual session.

However, there are counter arguments to be considered. The first is how effective it can be if individual family members enter into therapy reluctantly, or the whole family is not present. Another issue is that the therapist has to hold on to the view of the family as a single entity as well as seeing each person as an individual in his or her own right. This difficult balance makes it appropriate for therapists to work in pairs, or to be observed by others from behind a one-way screen. The necessary post-session discussion involved in both these ways of working can mean that for time and economic reasons, family therapy is only available for some families. Perhaps if this was not the case, fewer families would reach crisis or breakdown.

Allied to this is the sensitive issue of whether the family is the client, or the member who was the trigger for help being offered. Where do the needs of the child in the classroom fit into the general needs of the family? Is it always the case that by supporting the family and enabling them to live together more effectively that the emotional needs around education will be met?

Transactional analysis(TA)

Teachers working with children with special needs, and perhaps particularly their families, may find it useful to consider this approach which was originated by Berne, and whose book *Games People Play* (1964) has gained popular recognition. It is helpful to be aware at least of the concepts of Parent, Adult and Child. In TA terms, these are ego states which exist in all of us regardless of our chronological age or biological parenting. The Parent may be subdivided into Critical and Nurturing Parent, while the Child is divided into the Free Child and the Adapted Child, who may be Compliant or Rebellious.

It is essential to remember that all ego states are valuable; good or bad has no place in their definition. Disturbance may arise when there are conflicts between what an individual's Child wants and her Parent says she should want. There may also be conflict between people when one responds out of the Child to another's Parent, or indeed from any different state. The origins of the states are in our early experiences with significant others in our lives, but these have now become internalized into particular and sometimes habitual ways of responding.

TA is an approach which theorizes these transactions as a series of proactive and reactive options. Individuals, it is proposed, deal with each personal encounter in one of these three ego states. When their chosen approach is incongruent with that of the respondent, stress and distress occur. For example:

'Shall we have an ice cream/whisky?'
'You have one, but I don't feel like one just now' (Adult)

'Isn't it a bit soon after lunch?/Aren't you drinking rather a lot these days?' (Parent)
'Piggy!' (Adapted Child) 'Whoopee!' (Free Child)

The apparent, surface ego state may differ from the underlying psychological ego state. This means that people may behave and perceive the behaviour of others in one way at a surface level, but this may not actually reflect their underlying emotions. In order to maintain equilibrium in a social setting, people may hide their feelings, not only from others but also from themselves. Thus, a person caring for a cantankerous and perhaps dirty, senile old person, or an equally difficult child, may appear to act out of their Adult, or out of their Nurturing Parent, as a way of hiding their distaste and resentment, only to find that their feelings boil over eventually in an unacceptable way, perhaps out of the Rebellious Child or the Critical Parent. The object of the therapeutic encounter is for individuals to discover the way they habitually respond, and to enable them to react to one another from a more conscious state. In some cases this may resolve conflict; in others it may enable them to live with conflict and avoid escalating situations.

When we find ourselves thinking 'What did I say that for?' or 'Why am I responding like that?' it may well pay to see if we have hooked into our Parent, or Child state, or indeed into that of the other person involved. It is possible to diagnose our own state by analysing our behaviour, the reactions of others to it and our own history ('Gosh, I sound just like my mother did when I was ten and had a bad accident!).

When we consider the 'state' people are in, it can seem so obvious that it is easy to trivialize it. However, it can help us to understand and maybe unravel some of the issues which arise in relationships. It can also be a non-threatening way of explaining to others what is happening; it may allow them to stand back a little from the conflict, and also to work out for themselves their reasons for particular reactions. Again, it is not a magical cure, and it often takes time for our behaviours to catch up with our insights!

Creative therapies

The creative therapies cover a range of activities including drama, music, art and dance. There are professional artists who have trained to use their creativity therapeutically, such as art and music therapists, often working in residential or NHS settings. Others have a specific psychotherapy training which uses the art medium as a basis, and would include drama and art psychotherapists.

While not limited to use with any one client group, it is obvious that there is enormous value in using creative therapies with those who find it difficult to, or choose not to, communicate with words. Dance and drama therapy are, generally, group activities, while music and art are used with individuals and groups. Music has been effective with clients with whom there seemed to be no way to communicate. A young child who sat in an institutional setting repeatedly banging on a wall, was 'listened to' by a music therapist. She played out on a drum the simple rhythm he was making. Eventually, the boy seemed to become aware of this and responded to it, taking it in turns to 'talk'. From this repetition, he began to vary his response and take part in 'sound conversations'. This may not seem a very significant change, but this was in a child who had appeared unreachable. It was not a miracle cure and took a great deal of time and patience before he made any verbal communication. Musical instruments can also be used to enable clients to demonstrate or communicate how they are feeling.

Drawing, painting or modelling with clay can again be used to express an emotion or relive an experience. This can be solely through the medium, by enabling the client to demonstrate what is being felt, or by then talking about what has been created. In some approaches the therapist may interpret the art form in a similar way to an interpretation of a spoken statement. In others, clients are encouraged to say what it means for them and work with that.

A different way is to get the client to describe her creation and then to ask if any of the statements are true of herself. For example, if the client models or draws a boat, she might say that 'This is a small boat, being tossed in a storm, which is about to sink. There's no other boat around to rescue it, and its sails have been torn to pieces in the wind.'

The therapist might ask if it was possible to say, 'I am a small boat . . . There's no boat around to rescue me', to find out if this had meaning for the client. It may not have. On the other hand, it, could put the client in touch, as an example, with feelings of abandonment, fears of being overwhelmed by emotions or experiences, and having no one whom she trusts to help her through this. To uncover these feelings 'cold', a fairly articulate client is needed, so the art form has acted as an enabler. It is important to recognize that sometimes it can be enough for the client to have the experience and that no verbal follow-up is needed for insight or change to take place. There are occasions when the therapist may not know what is happening within the client, but the report back from home or school shows a change in behaviour or relating.

In group therapy, and sometimes in family therapy, use can be made of other people to 'sculpt' a situation or a feeling. This can again do away with the need for words. A child in conflict with the family may be asked if he would like to use other people to represent family members. They are placed as the sculptor wishes and will often demonstrate from where they have been placed in relationship to each other and in what sort of positions (crouching, contorted, on a table above the rest of the family) just what the client feels is happening, or how he relates to individuals in the group. Even when children (and adults!) know about the technique, and could be thought to be saying what they think they ought to say or avoiding things they do not wish to demonstrate, there is often unexpected insight. It is as if by using such techniques we can separate our selves and understand what it is that has been happening. Usually there has been little or no conscious awareness of this before the 'sculpt', although once we become aware, it may be as if it is something that we have known at some level. Perhaps we have buried it in our unconscious until that moment?

Play therapy is a very specific therapeutic way of working with children which also allows thoughts and feelings to be demonstrated with or without words. Interested readers are recommended to read Axline's *Dibs – In Search of Self* (1964), a moving account of her work with a six-year-old, or her classic book *Play Therapy* (1947) which has now been reissued as a paperback (1989).

It is thought that the creative therapies are effective because they break more quickly through defence mechanisms that have been built up by putting us in touch instinctively with our inner child.

Is therapy safe – and is it effective?

These are difficult questions to answer as in the end only the client knows. As long ago as 1977, Patterson said 'Anything goes in psychotherapy . . . . Every few months we have a new technique or approach being advocated . . . the evangelistic fervour with which many approaches are advocated . . . the failure to recognise that people can be hurt as well as helped' (Patterson, 1977, p. 19). More recently Masson (1990) has launched a swingeing attack on the whole field of therapy, claiming that 'the activity, by its very nature is harmful' and that in institutional settings therapists often impose a schedule and style of working which is contrary to the expressed wishes of the patient.

One of the difficulties in refuting Masson's view is in the limited research into the effectiveness of therapy. Thorne (1992, p. 17) comments on Rogers' work with seriously disturbed people in Wisconsin, which was evaluated at the time: 'In brief, the project did provide some solid support for Rogers' principal theories, but the overall findings were modest.'

Sutton (1989) comments that there have been few recent evaluated studies. She cites the work of Oldfield (1983) and Hunt (1985) and goes on to suggest that practitioners need to build in a simple means of evaluating the helpfulness of the service from the outset. Sutton is now working with Herbert on this in Leicester (Herbert, 1993).

While it would be foolish to pretend that malpractice does not ever occur, as in all professions, most therapists do seek to ensure that they work effectively and safely in a number of ways. Those entering therapy would do well to ask their prospective therapists about this, but it is recognized that this is easier to say than to do. Many clients feel powerless at the beginning of therapy and therefore are unlikely to ask the questions. One of the goals of most therapists is to try to ensure that the power in the relationship is evenly held, but this is rarely the case at the beginning.

One safeguard for the client is that the therapist is in supervision. In this context, this means that she meets regularly with someone as, or more, qualified than herself to consider issues arising from the therapeutic process. The functions of supervision are to help the therapist remain aware of what she is doing, including the risks, and to ensure that she remains open to learning. It is also a supportive encounter, though its prime aim is for the benefit of the client. Most therapists are also in ongoing therapy, and probably undertake further training from time to time. While membership of professional associations such as the British Association of Psychotherapists or the British Association for Counselling does not guarantee safe or effective working methods, at least it ensures adherence to a code of practice and a way of processing a complaint.

Crompton (1992) in her book on counselling children refers to Winnicott's concept of being 'good enough'. She is applying this to children who are in therapy and the difficulty they (and their families) have in seeing themselves as being, not perfect, but good enough. However, it could be applied to the whole therapeutic process. As Rowe reminds us in her introduction to Masson's book, 'All therapy works, but no therapy works perfectly' (Masson, 1990). In the majority of cases it is 'good enough'.

There is a dilemma around therapy and disability. On the one hand, it is not readily available and this can add stress to the individual and the family. On the other hand, in suggesting that it should be more available, one must be careful to be avoid being heard as saying that all people with disability, or their families, automatically need such support. Many will not, as in the general population.

As a postscript, it is acknowledged that many teachers, when working with children and their families, feel that they too are bordering on using therapeutic techniques. Indeed, within the person-centred and behavioural approaches, there may be considerable overlap. Some of the techniques of the creative therapies may already be in use or hold an appeal for the classroom teacher.

While recognizing that there are no clear demarcation lines, and that training is not always necessary to help people, it is worth remembering that they can be hurt as well. Interventions needs to be offered in such a way that it can be safely rejected, and teachers should be wary of using possible interpretations as if they were truths. There are many good short courses (ten to fifteen evenings) in counselling skills which would complement classroom approaches.

As has been emphasized for therapists, teachers also need support for their work, particularly where it borders on the therapeutic. It may not be provided in many schools, but there is nothing to prevent like-minded teachers getting together to obtain the support needed, so that they are less stressed by the work and the child is benefited indirectly.

Note

(1) The reader may be interested to note that the authors didn't always agree when constructing this section. One of us (SS) took a much more critical view of psychoanalysis and psychotherapy with people with severe learning difficulties; the other (AS), while not using this approach herself, was more inclined to see positive aspects to this way of working. The unresolved debate turned upon the matter of interpretation and explanation, SS taking the view that 'we should never accept a complicated explanation when a simple one would do' and AS that a simple explanation could not necessarily offer the best interpretation of an action, and that in any case a good therapist would already have examined and rejected such simplicities. Readers are invited to consider the matter for themselves.

For the reader

How can therapeutic approaches be understood by the teacher without resource to a 'blame the child' or 'blame the parent' model?' 'All actions have some meaning for the actor.' When using behavioural methods in the classroom, how much attention do you pay to the meaning of the action for the child? Can the reader examine the relationships in her own family and see how these may be productive or counterproductive? Arranging a selection of buttons from the button box to represent different family members can be very revealing.

6

He Understands every Word I Say:
The Speech and Language Therapist
Jannet Wright

Introduction: speech and language therapy and the health service
In 1969 a committee chaired by Professor Randolph Quirk was set up by the
Department of Education and Science (DES) and the Department of Health and
Social Security (DHSS) 'To consider the need for and the role of speech therapy
in the field of education and of medicine, the assessment and treatment of those
suffering from speech and language disorders and the training appropriate for
those specially concerned in this work and to make recommendations' (DES/
DHSS, 1972, p.iv).

At the time this report was commissioned there were two speech therapy
services: the education speech therapy service was part of the school health
service, and a hospital-based service formed part of the National Health Service
(NHS). There were about three times as many speech therapists employed in
the school health service as in the NHS.

When the Quirk Report was published (DES, 1972), the committee recommended in section 8.09 that 'the organisation of speech therapy services should
be unified', under area health authorities in England and Wales and health
boards in Scotland. Also that there should be a national adviser appointed to
the DHSS to assist the development of the speech therapy services.

In 1974 the speech therapy services in England and Wales became a unified
service within the NHS. Referrals to the service could be made by anyone
concerned about the development of a child's speech and language. Therapy
could take place in a variety of settings such as a health centre, a hospital or in a
school.

Colleagues in education frequently perceive speech and language therapists
as medical personnel. This is not only because the majority of therapists are

employed by the health service. But as Norwich (1990) states, the profession 'has a strong therapeutic or rehabilitative orientation with its immediate allied professions being medicine and other health service professions'.

This orientation is noticeable in the vocabulary of speech and language therapists. Words such as 'patient, diagnosis, prognosis or treatment' sound alien in a school but are commonplace when working in a hospital.

This alliance with the medical profession has historical roots as well as being perpetuated by the subject matter in the theoretical and clinical training of therapists.

The speech and language therapy service has always been managed within the health service. Knowledge gained from the field of medicine was very significant in the early history of the speech therapy profession, offering a systematic way of analysing a communication problem. The signs and symptoms of a particular communication problem are compared to others, already known, to arrive at a diagnosis. The therapist tries to establish the aetiology of a communication problem. The therapist will need to eliminate or reduce the influence of any organic factors such as a conductive hearing loss or unrepaired cleft palate, possibly by referral to a medically qualified professional.

A professional training course which covers a loss or slow development of communication skills due to brain damage, as a result of premature birth, infectious diseases, accident or degeneration, is bound to reflect this knowledge, both in approach to a problem and vocabulary. Colleagues see a link between medicine and speech and language therapy because they recognize the origin of some of the vocabulary. Other unfamiliar terminology used by the therapist is assumed to belong to the speech and language therapy profession. However, the profession has been influenced by other disciplines besides medicine, such as linguistics and psycholinguistics.

Phonology, semantics, syntax and pragmatics are terms used by speech and language therapists which come from the field of linguistics. The introduction of this area of study had an enormous impact on professional training and consequently on professional practice. Therapists now had the vocabulary and the knowledge to describe language development and breakdown. A range of assessment procedures was developed by linguists and therapists. However, the disadvantage of only using a linguistic approach to a child's communication problem is that psychological factors can be ignored, which is a major problem for those working with children.

A solution to this problem has been the introduction of a psycholinguistic model. This approach ensures that factors which influence the way a child learns are included in the evaluation of the child's communicative strengths and weaknesses. Both the linguistic structure and the psychological factors such as attention, perception and memory can all be considered. Then a holistic view of the child's communication skills can be taken.

Most speech and language therapists use a combination of all these approaches in their work. The complex nature of our human communication system requires therapists to acquire, synthesize and draw on the appropriate information to suit the individual needs of each client.

Education for speech and language therapy

There are two routes to a professional qualification as a speech and language therapist. The most popular route in the UK is still a three- or four-year undergraduate course. At graduation the successful student has a degree and a licence to practice from the professional body, the College of Speech and Language Therapists (CSLT). In 1991 the professional body changed its name. It had been the College of Speech Therapists, adding 'Language' was an attempt to represent accurately the work of the profession.

The second route which is becoming increasingly popular, is the two-year postgraduate course. The students cover the same subjects as those on an undergraduate course but in a shorter timescale.

All speech and language therapists training in the UK are qualified to work with both adults and children who have communication problems.

Newly qualified therapists often have a first job which involves working with both adults and children. A typical week would include time spent in a hospital with stroke patients, seeing children with severe learning difficulties in a special school and running an evening class for adults who stammer.

Communicating quality CSLT, (1991) describes three levels of professionally qualified therapists.

(1) Specialist speech and language therapists have additional qualifications, well-developed skills and an in-depth knowledge about a particular client group and/or a disorder. These therapists will act as advisers within the profession and to other related professional groups.

(2) Generalist speech and language therapists see a mixed population of clients. They will have good assessment, diagnostic and intervention skills but will not have acquired specialist knowledge of any particular group or disorder. They are not specialists.

(3) Specialized speech and language therapists: here specialization refers to a service provided to a single designated location, client group or those with a specific disorder. These therapists do not have the additional training or knowledge that a specialist

therapist has but they may work towards this in their professional development.

Therapists may also be able to work with speech and language therapy assistants. The assistants receive specific in-service training in order to do a variety of tasks ranging from preparation of equipment to carrying out certain therapy programmes. Sometimes an unpaid volunteer is involved in a variety of activities alongside the speech and language therapist.

Career progression within the profession has usually been based on some degree of specialization or a move into management. To specialize, a therapist would increase the amount of time spent with a chosen client group as well as receiving ongoing practical guidance from a more experienced/specialist therapist within that specialization. Attendance at in-service training courses would be expected and with increased specialization these courses are likely to be available only at a national level.

Communication difficulties in early childhood

A child's first words are a significant milestone for any parent. If a child's communication skills are limited or slow to develop, parents and professionals become concerned. A speech and language therapist is the appropriate professional to contact in this situation.

Most children enter nursery school or reception class with speech that other children and adults can understand. These children are able to listen and respond to both adults and other children.

Each child's communication style will vary a great deal at school entry. Some will have more to say than others and be more willing to volunteer information in a group; volume levels will vary as will the clarity of their speech. Differences such as these will be influenced by a child's previous experience as a speaker in the family or in preschool settings such as nurseries, mother and toddlers group, playgroup, their personality, the length of time in a particular class and the teaching style adopted by the adult in the classroom. All children will be different but most learn to talk without any difficulty and without causing concern to their family or teachers. However, some children do have difficulties learning to talk.

If children have a slight speech problem or even an unfamiliar accent, initially the listener may find them a little difficult to understand but will be able to adjust to their speech pattern fairly easily. These children have intelligible speech. In other cases the listener may not be able to make this easy adjustment and cannot understand what is said. Then a child is unintelligible to the listener. A child who is not understood by other children can become socially isolated and when adults do not understand the child they may look to the mother for a translation or say, 'he doesn't talk very well', 'what is she saying?', 'his speech isn't very clear is it?'

Children can be difficult to understand for a variety of reasons:

- the use of a limited range of speech sounds;
- a small vocabulary;
- difficulty finding the right word to express their thoughts;
- inability to remember the names of objects or people;
- problems in organizing the words they use into the expected grammatical order;
- problems with fluency;
- unexpected or inappropriate intonation patterns;
- problems co-ordinating breathing and speaking.

All or some of these reasons will contribute to a child's intelligibility. However, communication is not only about the structural aspects of language, it also includes the way people use their linguistic and their non-verbal skills.

A child may have a mature sound system, speak fluently in grammatical sentences and appear to have a wide vocabulary but still be described as a 'poor communicator'. This can happen if the way in which a child uses language, his pragmatic skills, is limited. In such a case a child may be unable to take turns in a conversation and so produces a monologue. He may assume that the listener has the same prior knowledge as he does and begin to recount a story in the middle, with few reference points. If a child has difficulties in the pragmatic aspects of language he may be unable to deal with anything presented in an abstract format. This extends into his appreciation of humour, where only the obvious and concrete humour of slapstick is understood and so produces laughter. If an adult uses sarcasm, it is lost on this child. He often responds only to the literal nature of such comments. This area of communication is the overlap between linguistic knowledge and social skills.

The child with a pragmatic problem often fails to understand the abstract aspects of language as well as the social nuances taken for granted in any classroom or social situation. But some children have difficulty understanding any aspect of spoken language.

Parents and teachers often believe that a child with a speech and language problem does understand 'everything that is said to him' and wonder why a speech and language therapist bothers to assess the child's verbal comprehension. Much of what is said to children by adults is accompanied by pointing, gesture and facial expression. This is particularly noticeable and appropriate in the early stages of language development; however, some children continue to rely on these non-verbal cues. If a child finds spoken language difficult to understand and struggles to make sense of the world around her she will copy other children. Often she will enjoy a routine that enables her to predict what will happen next. A child with a severe comprehension difficulty will reinforce that routine through rigid and sometimes extreme responses if anything unexpected happens.

The need to evaluate both spoken language as well as comprehension when a child is referred with a communication problem was reinforced by the research of Dorothy Bishop (1979, 1982). Prior to her research it had been thought that children could have expressive problems, without any comprehension difficulties. Bishop's work revealed that children with expressive language problems usually had some problems with comprehension. These findings confirmed that a speech and language therapist needs to assess all aspects of a child's communication ability.

Speech and language therapy and the education service

The medical orientation referred to by colleagues in education was reinforced with the Education Act 1981. When a speech and language therapist contributed to the full assessment procedure her report was summarized by the medical officer. This placed the therapist in the medical camp. It also sent clear messages about which government department was responsible for speech and language therapy services. Eventually, Circular 22/89 stated in para. 42 that advice about all therapy services provided by the district health authority (DHA) should be passed 'in full' to the local education authority (LEA) and attached as Appendix G (DES, 1989a).

The 'Lancashire ruling' (1989) stated that speech and language therapy can be considered as an educational provision or not as the individual circumstances indicate. The Education Reform Act 1988, Schedule 12, para. 83, enables LEAs to make non-educational provision, which could be speech therapy. If speech and language therapy is seen as an educational provision then there are significant implications for service delivery, teacher–therapist relationships and initial training. However, whether LEAs will be willing to fund speech therapy services which have previously been the responsibility of the health authority is still unclear.

Current ways of working

Conflicting interests influence the way speech and language services are delivered. There is pressure from the health authority managers to ensure that as many people as possible are seen each day. A health centre-based service is the easiest way of achieving this result. The therapist can then see several children in each session, a morning or afternoon. As it can take a whole session to visit one school to see a child and teacher, the pattern of service delivery which an administrator would favour is obvious.

The staff of the local schools usually take an opposite view. They prefer a school visit because a child with an appointment at the speech therapy clinic may miss half a day of school. In fact a therapist may prefer the school visit because then she can plan an intervention programme which is more relevant to the child's classroom activities.

Another reason for a speech and language therapist favouring school- or nursery-based intervention is non-attendance. A child offered therapy at a health centre is usually brought by his parent(s) or carers. Their involvement in the intervention process is crucial if a child's communication skills are going to improve. An isolated weekly appointment with the therapist will not produce any changes unless the intervention procedure is continued in the rest of their lives. However, other, more pressing demands may mean that the adult is unable to bring the child for therapy. Thus a therapist may book in several appointments during the day but unfortunately only two people attend. This is an unproductive and frustrating situation for the therapist. The children who fail to attend for speech and language therapy are probably the ones that both teacher and therapist are most concerned about.

Therapists have to discharge constant non-attenders to get through the list of other children referred for therapy. Unfortunately, as stated earlier, the children whom teachers are most concerned about are often those who fail to attend clinic appointments. In this situation a school-based service would seem to be a possible solution.

However, unless there is a group of children in one school the therapist could spend all her time travelling from school to school. A therapist in one clinic will be responsible for the preschool population with communication problems as well as at least eight to ten primary and secondary schools. The clinic therapist feeling frustrated by non-attendance may well be willing to offer such a service only to be thwarted by a manager who adopts a 'bums on seats' policy: that is if the speech therapists are not seen to be using their designated rooms in the health centre other staff such as the health visitor, school nurse, doctor or family planning staff will want to take them over. This situation is not one which most managers wish to encourage.

In response to pressures to ensure that children with statements for speech and language therapy receive adequate support some service managers have created new posts. These have been for therapists to support statemented children in mainstream schools. The therapist uses the clinic as an administrative base and spends most of the day in school. Such posts appear to be a positive response unless one suspects that they were created to reduce the risk of litigation against the DHA and the LEA.

In some speech and language therapy services the staff believe that the optimum period for language intervention is in the preschool years. Their aim is to reduce the number of older children who have communication problems. This means that the preschool population is seen as a matter of priority and the service to pupils in primary schools is reduced. With this model of service delivery there is a great reliance on the identification of children at risk of communication problems through the preschool health programme of developmental checks. It is also hoped that staff in day nurseries, playgroups and nursery classes and schools will also be able to identify and refer these children. However, there are always some children who slip through the net of developmental screening or preschool provision. They may not be identified until they have attended school for a period of time and then there may not be any support for them.

In schools, teachers are the permanent, consistent interactors with the child, the 'hosts'. The speech and language therapist may be a more transient figure. A therapist seeing a child at a health centre will, at best, hope for teacher co-operation in continuation in the classroom of work begun by the therapist. On the other hand, a school-based therapist has more opportunity than the teacher to develop good working practices towards jointly agreed goals for the child with communication problems.

Collaboration or consultation between teachers and therapists
'[I]n no way would I, as a parent, seek to usurp the skills of the professional, but it is my belief that in the field of special educational needs, of which I have experience, the professionals and the parents are mutually interdependent' (Da Costa, 1989). This parent, who has had considerable contact with teachers and speech and language therapists over his two language-impaired children, refers to a collaborative partnership. He is writing about a partnership between professionals and parents, but it is also necessary to ensure that such a partnership does exist between the professionals.

Speech and language therapists frequently use a consultancy approach to their work with other professionals. But this suggests a superior, 'expert' position not an interdependency. Spoken and written language is central to all aspects of the curriculum, both as the content and the medium of instruction. Therefore it would make sense for teachers and therapists to work collaboratively with children who have communication problems.

A survey was carried out to investigate whether this approach was in fact being used by speech and language therapists in England and Wales (Wright, 1992). Therapists were asked about the ways in which they collaborated with teachers when working with children who had communication problems. Two groups of therapists were contacted and were divided into two groups. There were those who were based in the same educational establishment as their teaching colleagues, such as a language unit or special school. And there were those whose base was a health centre. As one might have predicted, more school-based therapists had worked closely with teachers than had clinic-based therapists.

It became apparent from the responses of the speech and language therapists who were clinic based, that not all of them made contact with the child's teacher as a matter of routine. A teacher may not be aware of the possible educational problems that can be associated with communication difficulties. If she does not know that one of her pupils is attending speech and language therapy, how can she develop this knowledge? Also unless the teacher is aware that a child is about to start therapy, there is little possibility of a collaborative partnership developing between teacher and therapist. Speech and language therapists usually offer children a combination of some group and some individual therapy work. Children are withdrawn for therapy although the school-based therapists did work more frequently in the classroom than their clinic-based counterparts. When planning the intervention, half of the school-based therapists in this survey indicated that they planned the intervention with the teacher. Only a third of the clinic-based therapists shared the planning with the teacher.

It is in the intervention stage that the therapists believed that they collaborated most with the teachers. Although if the teachers have not been involved in the assessment or planning of an intervention strategy, they may feel little commitment or 'ownership' of a classroom-based intervention plan. This may make it difficult for them to prioritize this work.

It was surprising that collaboration only occurred over certain tasks. If collaboration, as defined by Conoley and Conoley (1981) is the 'joining together of two or more individuals in an egalitarian relationship to achieve a mutually determined goal' then the picture created by these responses is of consultation rather than collaboration. The teacher is the consultee who seeks advice and help from a consultant, the speech and language therapist. The 'specialist' assesses the child and plans the therapy. The therapists felt that they collaborated most at the time of intervention. So when do they work out their 'mutually determined goals', which therapists stated were an important motivation factor in the collaboration process?

Despite the speech and language therapists' selective pattern of collaboration they believed that collaboration with a child's teacher was important. They felt it was important to pool information – it increased their job satisfaction and helped their professional development. They also stated that it provided an effective outcome for the child.

To discover whether teachers held similar views, separate interviews were carried out with pairs of teachers and therapists, who worked together. Some pairs worked together in the same school or unit, in other pairs the therapist visited the school from a clinic base. All the professionals interviewed mentioned similar benefits as a result of collaboration as the therapists taking part in the survey. They were also clear about the personal and professional costs of working in this way. Therapists mentioned the cost of collaborating more frequently than did the teachers. Their comments included references to the physical cost and an acknowledgement of the 'loss' or need to relinquish some of one's own professional views and space:

> It is tiring, exhausting, it takes a lot out of you.
> You have to compromise.
> You give up what you regard as your domain.

The physical demands were echoed by the teachers as well as the balancing act required by a teacher in a busy classroom with many demands on her time:

> We work very hard at working together. Such close proximity puts a strain on you.
> It's another pull on your time.

If professionals adopt a collaborative working practice it implies an equality between them. In such a situation both may have to expose their ignorance and uncertainty as well as sharing information. Professionals have expectations of themselves and how they should behave. If someone feels that they are seen as inefficient or not fully informed, it becomes threatening. This vulnerability was recognized by both therapists and teachers:

> You lay yourself open when you say, 'I don't know what to do.'
> I did feel threatened to start with. I didn't want to appear completely stupid.

Teachers referred to the support offered through sharing concerns about an individual child. The interest and support of another professional with a different viewpoint can be a significant help: 'You can feel very isolated working with children like this and when I am on my own for the day there is nobody there to bounce ideas off.'

Therapists might assume that a teacher has considerable support from the rest of the staff in the school, when, in fact, the teacher feels that once the classroom door closes, he is on his own. Therapists and teachers acknowledged that during the partnership they had learnt a lot from the other person 'about literacy skills' – 'she's been a good role model for classroom language' – and recognized approaches that can be generalized – 'if it works with a supported child why shouldn't it work with the others.' This cognitive gain highlights the useful sharing which could go on between these two professionals for the benefit of more children.

What can we share?

Therapist and teacher need to be aware of the differences between them as well as having an awareness of the similarities. This would enable them to work more effectively together.

A common vocabulary would make it easier to share skills. So the needs of each individual child would be identified by both parties through a joint assessment. Some tasks can be done by a specific person, for example the therapist would probably be more familiar with a linguistic or phonological assessment and the teacher is better placed to look at how the child uses language in the classroom and carry out an assessment of the child's numeracy or literacy.

There is also a strong argument for enabling both teachers and therapists to identify what they already do to help children with communication problems, then considering how these strategies can be used or enhanced in a classroom. It might involve looking at what strategies a child uses in order to get help in the classroom or reducing the linguistic complexity of a classroom instruction.

Should trainee teachers and therapists learn this approach during their initial training, as David and Smith (1987) recommend, or at post-qualification stage? By this time the individual has begun to feel comfortable with her new professional identity. However, the main problem with working at a post-qualification level is that children with communication problems can arrive in the classroom of any teacher, even if it is her probationary year, and the local speech and language therapist may also be newly qualified. This suggests that something needs to happen in the training period to prepare teachers and therapists for a collaborative style of work. This should then be re-evaluated after some time in work. With teacher training currently undergoing so many changes, is this yet another pressure on the trainers organizing the timetable? Is the speech and language therapist just one of many potential professional partners with whom teachers have to interact?

Perhaps it is more a matter of helping embryonic professionals to recognize their own strengths and limitations, as well as enabling them to become as skilful as possible in any professional partnership.

Conclusion

The research quoted earlier in this chapter was started because there was a lack of information about how therapists and teachers did work together, if at all. It appears that therapists support the approach even if it is not always translated into practice, and also that increased contact with schools is a good thing, although teachers need to be aware that speech and language therapists may have been involved with a child long before he enters the school system.

Teachers and therapists operate within totally different systems. They are both specialists in their knowledge of these systems and need to become aware of the demands and potential of their partner's system. Therapists' unique assessment skills and knowledge can be helpful to any client group. They can be utilized in a school setting and shared with teaching colleagues. Teachers have a tremendous opportunity to help children with their language structure as well as its use. If these two professionals can share at least some of their information and expertise to respond to the needs of each individual child we will offer a service which has flexibility and room for growth.

For the reader

Think about your own classroom practice and consider how far you take the opportunity identified in the last paragraph to help with language structure and use.

Case Reference

R. v. Lancashire County Council *ex parte* C. M. 1989.

7

Unsung Heroes: Other Paramedical Specialisms

Sarah Sandow

In the previous chapter Jannet Wright examined the special role of one of the paramedical professions with a particular interest and approach to special educational needs. In this chapter, the part played by two other 'professions supplementary to medicine' will be considered: the occupational therapist and the physiotherapist. These two groups have a great deal in common. Each is a twentieth century foundation built upon ancient traditions. Each plays a part in the treatment and rehabilitation of individuals of all ages including those with mental or physical disorders. Each has recently become a 'graduate-entry' profession, and each is threatened by recent developments in the health service and the economic constraints of the 1990s. Each group has also developed skills and interests beyond those with which it was traditionally associated and, in doing so, the clear definition of roles has become blurred. Nevertheless, both occupational therapists and physiotherapists have a particular approach to special educational needs, which will be explored here.

The occupational therapist
Looking at the range of activities and skills practised by the occupational therapist today, it may appear that the roles of the occupational therapist and of the psychotherapist or counsellor, discussed in Chapter 5, overlap as many of the activities are common to both. Each may engage with children in play therapy, art, music or drama, and each tends to be involved in individual encounters with 'patients' or 'clients'. To explore the difference, it is necessary to take a long view. Occupational therapists have developed a professional philosophy which is rooted in the 'moral model' discussed in Chapter 1, though some would argue that its origins are even older. Hopkins and Smith (1971) cited the integration of a healthy body, mind and spirit as

characteristic of the philosophies of ancient civilizations. This integration was to be achieved by activity as well as by thought. In the eighteenth and early nineteenth centuries, 'moral treatment' was applied for the first time to the mentally ill. The York Retreat was one of the first asylums where a moral regime was introduced. Before this time, it had been thought that the only treatment was to frighten or physically abuse the patient, perhaps in a vain attempt to 'drive out the devils', at a time when mental illness was equated with possession. There was, of course, considerable difficulty about the distinction between the mentally ill and the handicapped[1]. Moral treatment included not only a more sympathetic and supportive regime, but also the inculcation of habits of work and occupation not too different from those which obtained in normal life. Bockoven (1972) has described moral treatment as having four elements: first, the inculcation of positive affect, including confidence, enthusiasm and hope as opposed to the sense of despair and helplessness which are characteristic of depressive illness; second, the idea that, there was a morality about normal behaviour (within any social context), that is that ordering one's life in accordance with a recognized system of 'mores' promoted a sense of well-being; third, that mental illness was just that, an illness, and not a form of moral degeneration which was the responsibility of the patient; and fourth, 'moral treatment' referred to the responsibility of the carer to look after the invalid and not to abuse him as previously.

The contrast between this approach and the chains of Bedlam may be imagined. Therapeutically, it was the task of the carer so to fill the time and the emotions of the patient with positive experiences that there was no room for despair, and thus to establish patterns of activity which gradually became habitual.

Moral treatment was a great success and enormously improved the lives and prospects of many of the mentally ill. Unfortunately it did not last long. As in other areas, it was superseded by a medical model compounded by the Social Darwinism which accepted and promoted inequality as a natural order. The new medical interpretations of mental illness identified it as a disease of the brain for which there could be no cure or amelioration. The rapidly increasing population, especially of the poor, at a time of minimal social provision, with a concomitant increase in mental illness and disability, meant that the policy of treatment was gradually replaced by a policy of containment. Great mental hospitals were built, usually in the countryside, away from population centres, to reduce the possibility of contamination and miscegenation. The inmates were a combination of the insane, the idiots and the imbeciles.[2] Their occupations, where they had any, were repetitive domestic tasks and their exercise consisted of hours spent walking in circles round the 'airing courts' provided for that purpose.

Moral treatment went into abeyance until twentieth century occupational therapy began with the work of those such as Meyer (1922) and Slagle (1922) who revived the idea that the development of habits of meaningful occupation was essential to the maintenance of health. The important thing about this approach was (and remains) that the occupation is not simple diversionary busyness which takes place merely as a backdrop to more important psychotherapeutic treatment; it is seen as essentially therapeutic in its own right. It links the individual with his or her environment. Thus, play therapy is not simply a means to enable the patient and the therapist to explore unuttered emotions, it has an intrinsic value as ordered activity which leads the patient towards normality.

Colleges of occupational therapy were founded in the 1920s and 1930s, including the London College of Occupational Therapy which began in 1935 with six students. This and other colleges and schools attached to hospitals offered diplomas to an increasing number of students, but permission to run degree courses was not granted until 1988, significantly later than in many other countries. By 1990 there were more than 10,000 occupational therapists.

Within the hierarchical structure of the health services, it was hard for occupational therapy to maintain its basic philosophical stance. The training was conducted until the 1980s within a largely medical framework, although from the late 1960s the then Association of Occupational Therapists was urging a more liberal curriculum. A central problem, however, was, and is, the evaluation of occupational therapy techniques. The desired end product, the well-adjusted individual, is hard to identify, and even harder to relate to a specific therapeutic activity. Accountability, seen increasingly in terms of technical outcomes, cannot easily be applied to a process which is variable, which embraces a wide range of activities and which is tailored to the individual patient. Seeking to be a profession complementary to medicine with its own philosophy, principles and methodology, occupational therapy is often seen instead as one of a number of professions supplementary to medicine, and the utilization of its skills has depended on factors outside the control of the profession.

One of these has been the psychoanalytic approach to mental illness which prevailed in the decades following the 1930s. A view of mental illness obtained in which patients were perceived as needing to express, primarily through talk but also through activity, those repressed emotions and anxieties which were preventing them from maturing and developing normal relationships. In this context, occupational therapists developed methods by which crafts could be used to reveal emotions and symbolic themes and as methods for working out themes and conflicts, as well as to receive gratification at regressed levels of psychosexual development. However, this approach to occupational therapy has been criticised as both abandoning the field's original mission to use occupation to organise behaviour and as selling short the real value of occupation. Thus it has been challenged by therapists for being in opposition to both the development of a unique identity for the profession of occupational therapy and to the original tenets of the field. The use of activities as a means of expressing unconscious material and pent up emotions directly contradicts the use of activities to challenge and promote adaptive behaviour.

(Barris, Kielhofner and Watts, 1983, p. 27)

Today, in the hands of some psychotherapists and clinical psychologists, occupations such as painting, music-making or horticulture are seen as means to the end of self-analysis and self-understanding. Perhaps there is a place for this (see Chapter 4); but it is not true occupational therapy within the meaning outlined above. In response to this approach, some occupational therapists began to theorize more explicitly the work they undertook. Yerxa (1983) proposed a series of principles, as follows:

(1) Humans are to be viewed as self-directed.
(2) All persons have the right to the highest quality of existence.
(3) Humans are multifaceted complex systems that interact with the environment and accumulate subjective experiences.
(4) The therapeutic process is an interaction between client, therapist and environment.
(5) Health is a dynamic balance of leisure, self-maintenance and productive participation in society.

These statements emphasize the centrality of the individual patient, who in seeking 'health' and 'quality of life' does so in a way which is described as 'self-directed'. That is to say that the occupational therapist desires to work in a holistic way, designing programmes with the co-operation of the individual in clear relation to his or her needs. They are in sharp contrast to the traditional view of the occupational therapist imposing a regime of basket-making or printing on a group of patients without reference to individual needs. The list of principles is reminiscent of Maslow's self-actualization, for example, and the developing self-advocacy movement (see Chapters 7 and 8) is also relevant. The 'dynamic balance' has echoes of much stress management technology. It is also notable that the emphasis is on the interaction, not only between the individual and the environment, but between the 'client, therapist and environment'; thus Yerxa is laying claim to being more than an initiator or catalyst for change.

If this dynamism was threatened by psychoanalysis, which sought to lay bare the thought processes and emotions of the patient rather than to obscure them, it is also currently threatened by economics. What has been described here is a holistic person-centred process. Current practitioners, here and on the Continent, for example at the Institute Sint-Vincentius in Belgium, seek to encourage client-directed programmes in which the autonomy of the individual is promoted. Such programmes engage the client and therapist in a productive relationship with the environment which cannot work without a full understanding of the relation of practice to theory. However, within the NHS today, this once coherent philosophy has an uncertain future. Diminishing resources, reduced staffing levels with limited professional supervision (Correia, 1993), the relocation of occupational therapy within a medically directed framework (most clinics are headed by doctors), the blurring of professional responsibilities, cutbacks in the child health service, all lead to confusion and disintegration. There is a high burn-out rate for the, usually young, usually female (and therefore underpaid) professional. All of these may result in what Turner (1987) has called the proletarianization of professions. This is characterized by a diminution of the control exercised by the professional over how, when and where she operates, and which reassigns her to a role, not as a partner to other professionals but as a servant carrying out limited and time-constrained operations.

The effect of this on the way occupational therapists work with teachers, parents and children could be very destructive. Within the clinic it is still possible to operate to some extent within a holistic framework, but it is more likely that advice will be sought in the clinic, and certainly in the school, on a particular aspect of behaviour or development, such as clumsiness, balance, handwriting, or some other specific problem. Assessment and reassessment, using a range of tests, are the foundations of remedial activity, with children as with adults, but these processes take more time than is usually available. As the object of the exercise is not simply rehabilitation, but adaptation to circumstances such that normal or near normal activity can take place, the piecemeal treatment of a condition rather than an individual runs counter to the professional philosophy.

Occupational therapists work extensively with adults with special needs, carrying out programmes designed to establish basic-, intermediate- and advanced-level living skills, which enable individuals to maintain themselves in the community. As the new community care legislation takes effect, they expect to be more heavily involved in this work. Many of these programmes are similar to those which form a large part of the curriculum in special schools for sixteen- to nineteen-year-olds. They include shopping, household management, personal hygiene and care, and social skills. It is difficult to identify at this level the difference between teaching and therapy, and this may cause both teachers and therapists to feel unclear and uncomfortable about the boundaries of their roles.

Within schools, occupational therapists are working within an external, curricular framework, which has its own logic and its own requirements. The occupational therapists in the school may find themselves adapting to a subordinate role in which their original commitment to a professional philosophy of occupational health is lost in a range of apparently unconnected, eclectic exercises with a range of pupils. Even though teachers will be glad to welcome assistance with children who are clumsy, socially or physically incompetent, or displaying inappropriate behaviour, sorting out the responsibilities and roles may be problematic. However, given the therapists' special training in diagnosing, managing and alleviating problems such as these, collaborative work is clearly indicated. Occupational therapists may also be able to give information and advice on special conditions such as sickle-cell anaemia, the management of children with life-threatening illnesses such as leukaemia, or degenerative diseases such as muscular dystrophy. Where the therapist treats the child outside the school in a clinic, the problems of communication between the two professionals may be more complicated as the opportunities for information exchange may be limited. Working within the context of the National Curriculum, teachers will find it more and more difficult to devote time to those aspects of common interest, such as hyperactivity, perceptual motor development or play, however important these may be for individual children.

So is it possible to identify a specific view of special educational needs on the part of the occupational therapist? We have seen that the classical view is represented by the moral model, although the opportunities for fully applying this model are diminishing. Working within a medical framework, and deeply influenced by associated therapies, it is hard for occupational therapists to avoid the deficit view inherent in the medical model. It remains to be seen whether the person-centred holistic approach will be allowed to win through in the next decade. For teachers, there is a special responsibility to facilitate a positive relationship with this other profession, with whom they share similar concerns, to promote the good of the children they both serve.

Physiotherapy

It is easier in many ways to identify the place of the physiotherapist in relation to the client and to other professionals. There are a number of reasons for this.

First, physiotherapists possess a highly specialized body of knowledge respected by other professionals and clients. They have a clearly identified unambiguous function. Whereas the lay view of the occupational therapist is of someone equipped to amuse with baskets and jigsaw puzzles, the curative role of the physiotherapist is seen publicly in the context of sports injuries, recovery from accidents and the treatment of back pain. In the latter case, particularly, the effect may appear miraculous. The physiotherapist thus shares with the doctor the reputation of being able to cure, through the application of special skills unavailable to others.

Secondly, just as lay people would hesitate to prescribe medication (other than in simple matters) for themselves or their children, because it is recognized that mistakes can be made, so also it is recognized that amateur physiotherapy can be disastrous. Because 'the wrong treatment' is visibly possible, the accountability of the physiotherapist is also visible, in a way which cannot be said of the occupational therapist.

Third, the relationship between physiotherapists and doctors is not unequal: patients are referred to chartered physiotherapists by doctors who recognize the specialist knowledge and skill of fellow professionals, whom they trust to take responsibility for independent decision-making in the implementation of a treatment programme (DHSS Circular 77/33). Physiotherapists and doctors share a professional language, though they will approach problems from a different angle.

Finally, teachers and others are aware that the client or patient served by the physiotherapist belongs to a group most vulnerable and least disapproved of all children with special needs: those with physical handicaps. It is not surprising therefore that those who treat this group receive concomitant respect.

Physiotherapy is also an ancient skill, established in this century as a professional activity. It derives from the Chartered Society of Masseuses and Remedial Gymnasts, founded in 1920, which did not change its name to the Chartered Society of Physiotherapists until 1943. Its original aim was to 'improve the training, education and professional status of persons engaged in the practice of massage, medical gymnastics and electrotherapeutics or kindred methods of treatment and to foster and develop the use of these and kindred forms of treatment'. Physiotherapists since that time have gradually extended their activities as techniques of remediation have multiplied. Many began asking the question, 'What is physiotherapy?' (Peat, 1981; Walton, 1990) and some have felt that the clear focus of their activities has become occluded. Williams (1986) has also recognized the problems of definition which must be solved if the profession is to survive in the 1990s. For lack of a clear alternative, she wrote, a medical model could be imposed externally, leading young physiotherapists to think in terms of pathology, rather than about restoring function and ability. Williams stressed the importance for the profession of 'handling' the patient, and remarked that this aspect of the work, unique to physiotherapy, is not given enough recognition even by physiotherapists themselves.

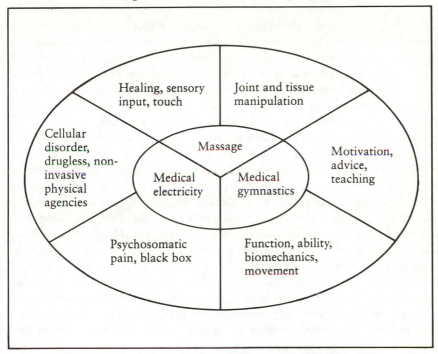

Core skills of the physiotherapist, from Williams, J. I. (1986) Physiotherapy is handling, *Physiotherapy*, Vol. 72, no. 2, pp. 66–70.

The 'core skills' – massage, medical gymnastics and medical electricity and their extensions (see figure) – comprise art as well as science:

> a manual art that is our core and very important. Because we were told that we were not evaluating our work and that we were not doing research, we thought only scientific things counted . . . . Physiotherapists know with their hands. They learn with their hands. It is extremely difficult for them to express what they know.
>
> (Williams, 1986, p. 68)

Many physiotherapists feel that the transmission of this 'manual knowledge' is under threat from the recent elaboration of training courses into degree-level studies, and the resulting withdrawal of courses from hospitals to universities. This has meant that teachers of physiotherapy now concern themselves more with theory and information, and the practical induction of students in hospitals is now the responsibility of clinical supervisors.

Blythe (1985) discussed the use of physiotherapy with those with learning difficulties, pointing out the increased incidence in this population of medical problems such as chest conditions, obesity, spasticity, overextension and skeletal abnormalities. She points out that in assessment, the patient may not be able to complain of pain or explain his feelings. He may also display heightened apprehension, and may depend more than most on seeing the same therapist. Unusual gait patterns, compensation to avoid discomfort, pallor, cyanosis or hyperventilation will be observed by the physiotherapist, who will consider the patient's ability to climb stairs or use a bath. She will weigh the advantages, disadvantages and the ethical implications of using splints or helmets to prevent self-injury. She will collaborate with orthopaedic specialists in the provision and monitoring of prostheses. She will consider and recommend which of a wide range of wheelchairs, standing frames or prone boards may be appropriate. Other aspects which may be reviewed include eating skills, eye–hand co-ordination, adapted eating utensils, personal hygiene, continence, easily fastened clothing and footwear. Physical exercise and massage for cerebral palsied children or for sickle-cell disease and chest clearing in cystic fibrosis also form part of her responsibility. Hydrotherapy, for recreation, relaxation and pain-free movement, is in increasing demand, and many special schools now have their own hydrotherapy pool. It is clear that the list is lengthening and perhaps begins to overlap the interests of occupational therapists. Again we see a blurring of roles between groups of apparently competing professionals. It is also clear that this extensive list moves far beyond the original core of massage, remedial gymnastics and medical electricity.

The physiotherapists' model of special needs looks superficially very like a medical model. Physiotherapists themselves prefer to talk of 'disorders' rather than 'disease'. As Williams indicated, they will clear the throat of the patient, not worry about reducing the temperature. Similarly when considering the special needs of the child, they are concerned to make the world accessible for him and seek to modify the environment and soothe the discomfort, to make this possible.

New directions
In the late 1980s there were moves to combine degree courses for occupational therapy and physiotherapy. The College of Occupational Therapists set up an independent commission to examine the present and future role of the profession chaired by Louis Blom-Cooper. The report (COT, 1989) considered the arguments for and against combining the two specialisms. Although several advantages were cited, including the overlap between functions, the similarities in training, employment logistics and the problems of competition, the commission rejected a conjoined rehabilitation service, mainly it seems on

the grounds of possible disruption and of sentiment. Interestingly, however, the report did not discuss in detail any of the philosophical issues which have been mentioned above, and which do effectively differentiate the professions. The probability is increasing, however, especially in community care programmes, that occupational therapists and physiotherapists will find it hard to retain their distinct entities. It is unlikely that in a domiciliary service, a range of professionals will be employed to support one patient. It is more likely that assessments of need will result in a policy of 'best fit', where one or other of the available peripatetic staff will manage the patient. Both professions are afraid of a resulting dilution of skill and generalization of practice (Correia, 1993).

An associated current issue for both professions is the 'borrowing' of techniques, either by other professionals, quasi-professionals or amateurs. Foot massage, aromatherapy or other techniques may be delivered in a perfectly proper way by the unqualified, but there are dangers. With respect to children or adults with special needs, we have to ask ourselves whether the severely handicapped individual is in a position to object when his teacher, say, decides that she knows how to use massage? Can the provision of sensory experience in the form of noxious-tasting substances designed to alert the senses (mustard or chilli, for example) be said to be an assault? It is less likely that the teacher or carer will have considered this, and less likely that she will be as alert to signs of distress or rejection as those trained to be so.

A paradox

Turner (1987) has suggested that all professions display a tension between indeterminacy (also called by Schon (1983) 'professional artistry') and technicality. This is a reflection of the 'opposition between technical and routine knowledge and the ideology or mystique of interpretation. As a result we can conceptualise professions as occupations subject to contradictory forces which simultaneously push them towards proletarianism and professionalism' (Turner, 1987, p. 138) It is useful to compare occupational therapy with physiotherapy in the context of this statement. Occupational therapy is perceived by its practitioners as possessing a high degree of indeterminacy, but is being pushed by circumstances towards proletarianization. On the other hand, physiotherapy is seen as containing a high proportion of technical–rational knowledge (so much so that Williams (1986) a distinguished therapist, was driven to write begging the profession to remember its artistic centre) but is recognized by the public and by other health practitioners as highly professional. While Williams was resisting the scientific research focus, the Blom-Cooper Report was recommending to the College of Occupational Therapists that it should 'seek to validate the profession's claims to professional status by devising ways of measuring and monitoring the effectiveness and efficiency of practices, procedures and organisational arrangements' (COT, 1989, p. 88).

It appears that both professions are caught between two stools, needing to be seen as technical–rational occupations for survival in the age of the performance indicator, but struggling to retain their professional artistry. For teachers, their dilemma will be a familiar one.

Acknowledgement
I am grateful for the advice of Bernadette Waters and Jennifer Mizon during the writing of this chapter.

Notes
(1) As there was well into this century. The writer recalls, in the 1960s, working in a particular large mental hospital where, following the 'unlocking of doors' in 1958, large numbers of adults were transferred to the neighbouring hospital for the mentally handicapped, only just having been recognized as such.

(2) These were the 'scientific' descriptors of the time.

For the reader
Try to find an occupational therapist or physiotherapist and discuss with them the rationale for their work. Does it echo what has been written here?

Introduction to Chapters 8 and 9

The two following chapters have several things in common. Each represents a view derived from an academic discipline. Philip Garner writes from a sociological perspective, Viv Hinchcliffe's chapter reflects aspects of developmental psychology. Both disciplines are currently unfashionable in an educational world in which teachers are encouraged to a simpler, more directive approach to their task. In each case, this instrumental view is criticized as an inadequate response to a complex situation. In each case the contribution of the student or pupil with special educational needs is identified. 'Child-centred' education is now derided, but only by asking questions of the student or by detailed observation can the experience of education be understood from the point of view of the recipient. In each chapter it is argued that designing and interpreting a curriculum without reference to the child, and applying it regardless of the child's actual or potential contribution, devalues the educational process.

Garner looks first at the way sociologists have identified the concomitants of educational failure, and have sought to persuade teachers to look at the inadequacies of the offered curriculum rather than the incompetences of the students. In this context he describes the responses of some 'disruptive' students to their education, and finds that their views correspond more than one might expect to those of other educational 'consumers'.

Hinchcliffe looks at self-advocacy among children with severe learning difficulties and identifies ways in which some of the barriers to participation in the learning process can be broken down, by observation, analysis and synthesis of vital psychological processes.

Both chapters demonstrate the inadequacy of a simple didactic approach and, in doing so, remind us that the students themselves present a model of special needs which is as valid as any of the others described in this volume.

8

It's all Society's Fault: Sociology and Special Education

Philip Garner

Sociology, or the study of people in groups, has generally had a very bad press during the last fifteen years or so. In part this has been a result of what some have regarded as the influence of 'the disgracefully sloppy thinking of the nineteen sixties' (Marsland, 1992). But it appears not to be a coincidence that this period has coincided with the dominance of right-wing political thinking, in both the UK and the USA. To politicians, whose ideological persuasions are rooted in free choice and the power of the market-place, a sociologist was often seen as a thorn in the side of this new(er) establishment. In a sense this may be regarded as one result of the aftermath of the rather loose, intellectually incoherent dogmas of the 1960s and 1970s. The axiom appears to be that those whose ideologies are rooted in the beliefs of a so-called permissive generation must be academically permissive themselves.

In any case, what is the point of sociology? Does it not merely confirm what we already know? The familiar territories of 'cycles of disadvantage', labelling and self-fulfilment, underpinned by equality issues, have resulted in a 'depressing picture of the extent and stubbornness of inequalities' (Barton and Oliver, 1992, p. 67). The debate has been well rehearsed and the polar views of the two 'sides' in this dogfight have come to be characterized as a quest by trendy liberals to destabilize an existing order, which has seen teachers and educationists as enemies of traditional values, based upon individuality, excellence and competition.

Within education such a vignette is especially apparent and it is particularly so in special educational needs. From the 1970s onwards it is accurate to suggest that teachers in schools, and education in general, have been frequently used as scapegoats for all manner of societal problems. Most recently in February 1993, the Secretary of State for Health reportedly remarked that 'We must challenge the indifference of teachers and social workers and the do-gooders who don't'.

In this chapter, however, I do not wish to dwell too much on such arguments: they have been adequately rehearsed elsewhere (Chitty, 1989). Rather, I wish to present a more optimistic interpretation of the role of sociology as it relates to special educational needs. By doing this I hope to suggest that an interest in micro-sociology of schools and classrooms may lead to a re-establishment of the important links between educational performance and societal inequality in relation to those students who are regarded as disruptive. The suggestion I intend to make is that continued recognition of this interface is essential if individual and institutional practices are to be refined in order to deal more effectively with the problems that such students pose for teachers.

I intend to do this in three ways, and with specific reference to those school students whose special educational needs concern their inappropriate behaviour in school. In the first part of the chapter I will examine the contribution of sociology to the theory and practice of this aspect of special education and briefly sketch its relevance to teachers in schools. This will suggest that studies of the societal context of disruptive behaviour have tended to present a deterministic and deficit interpretation, and that only recently have micro-studies, focusing upon the power of 'agency' (Shilling, 1992), started to play an important and proactive role in actively influencing what goes on in classrooms and schools.

This interpretation is based upon a micro versus macro theoretical paradigm. In this a tension is seen between sociological theories which have been applied to society at large (for example, the Marxist belief that a theory of 'correspondence' obtained in education and the workplace) and those which have been adopted for use in a much more restricted setting (for example, the use by Woods (1979) of the notion of a 'pedagogy of survival' in schools and classrooms).

The second part of the chapter will endeavour to illustrate the value of such micro-sociological approaches to teachers, using the example of one small-scale case study of so-called disruptive students. This will demonstrate that by inquiring into the micro-sociology of the school teachers can obtain important information which will, ultimately, make their task of teaching at least a little more straightforward, whilst at the same time ensuring a more rewarding experience for the school students. In the final part of the chapter I will seek to project the lessons learned from this type of exercise, so that they may be viewed as more central to the work that we do with those children who have special educational needs.

Is it all society's fault?

There is a long, and fairly depressing, literature concerning the nature of environmental effect on the educational opportunities of children and the relationship of these to those students whose behaviour in school interferes with their learning and results in them being categorized as having special educational needs (Rutter and Madge, 1976; Essen and Wedge, 1982b). Nowhere is this relationship more apparent than in the metropolitan areas of England (Bash, Coulby and Jones, 1985). What is clear from much of this writing is that the parameters of race, gender, social class and political and economic status all have some part to play in explaining the spatial location of the majority of children who have behavioural difficulties in certain schools: this location is primarily in particular urban areas, where the indices of disadvantage are most apparent. Whilst this is not to say that there are not similar cases in what may be termed more benign environments (Adams, 1991), the literature does illustrate the essential selectivity of the incidence of this aspect of special educational needs, according to a range of environmental factors. These had been noted in deficit terms by Castle, who remarked that 'In urban situations where social stability and tradition are weakest . . . where slum conditions provide no stable basis for home discipline, where classes are larger and buildings inadequate . . . [teachers] are faced daily with disciplinary difficulties hardly known to their more fortunate colleagues' (Castle, 1958, p. 368).

Whilst emphasizing the link between environment and disruptive behaviour, it is also important to remain aware of the relationship of these two to the learning progress of students. Sociologists have been able to provide overviews of these environmental links, so that educational policy and practice may be adjusted to accommodate them. It is widely acknowledged, for instance, that those school students who are inclined to behave badly, to such an extent that they assume the descriptor of 'disruptive student', are also, in most cases, students who experience learning difficulties. Lake (1991), researching reading failure, noted that certain societal factors, including social class, characterized the failing reader.

Two recent government publications illustrate the use of the concept of environmental effect quite graphically; both have relevance to the position of disruptive students in schools. In the case of learning progress, the Department for Education (DfE) published, for the first time (late 1992), 'league tables' of the performance of seven-year-olds in National Curriculum tests in English, reading, maths and science. The tables showed a marked spatial differentiation between the performance of schools in those local education authorities serving some of the most socially and economically disadvantaged communities in certain urban areas and those in what may be termed 'privileged' or middle-class regions. The former are those urban communities from which the 'disruptive' population is largely drawn. Of course, exceptions abound, but the general rule appeared to be that educational performance is in a substantive way related to life chances.

A second document, relating to exclusions from schools, was also published at about the same time (November 1992). This contained a bleak summary of data obtained from the National Exclusions Reporting System (NERS), which was inaugurated in 1990 to monitor the incidence of permanent exclusions. This shows that 12.5 per cent of those excluded held statements of special educational need, that Afro-Caribbean pupils appeared to be disproportionately represented within the excluded population, and that boys rather than girls were far more prone to exclusion. From available research we are aware that the special-needs population in schools is located mainly in urban areas, as also are substantial numbers of black pupils. Add to that the evidence that of the special-needs population it is boys rather than girls who predominate, and a picture begins to be formed of a set of interdependent factors within society which forms a basis for developing an understanding of the location of children who have special educational needs in certain areas of large towns and cities. The unifying theme appears to be social and economic disadvantage. The Center on Evaluation, Development and Research (1981, p. 5) provides an apt summary of this state of affairs: 'Research to identify potentially disruptive students has isolated dozens of variables: socio-economic status, academic achievement, IQ, race, sex, age, number of siblings and whether or not parents are divorced.'

Those studying the way in which these discrepancies have been used to interpret the way that society in general and educational systems in particular are structured have often been criticized. I propose that a major reason for this is fear, rooted in a mistrust of anyone who wishes to challenge or change the social order, so that equality of opportunity may be made more attainable to those groups of society who are marginalized. My interpretation is that sociologists, discounting their personal and often left-wing ideologies, have often presented powerful arguments to explain why and to what extent society contributes to both the creation, and the spatial location, of children who have special educational needs. In this sense, the macro-theoreticians may be seen as rather more of a threat to order than more small-scale interpretations investigating the micro-sociology of schools – a point to which I will refer later in this chapter.

Sociological analysis of special education *per se* is a relatively new development in England (Barton and Oliver, 1992). But within a comparatively short time there has developed a tradition of enquiry by sociologists working in the field of special education into questions of, amongst other things, social control, the social construction of categories of special need, deficit orientations, and the ideology of professionals engaged in special education. Often, however, these have been used as a means of establishing theoretical insights into macro-features of society rather than highlighting practical issues relevant to teachers in classrooms. Notwithstanding this, the influence of the work of writers like Tomlinson (1982), Ford, Mongon and Whelan (1982) Barton and Tomlinson (1984), Fulcher (1989) and Arnot and Barton (1992) has been important in raising the awareness of the role that sociology could play in understanding how and why education systems respond as they do to those who have special educational needs.

The problem of respectability thus encountered by sociologists has, I believe, an important bearing upon the attitudes of both educational professionals and others to the influences that environmental factors have on the creation of a special educational need. Even teachers, often in the past such bastions of support for the notions of inequality and disadvantage, have tended to become cynical or distrustful of anyone who suggests that society at large, including schools, has an important part to play in establishing or reinforcing learning or behavioural difficulty: witness the withering looks on school training days when such things are mooted. One explanation is that from the 1980s onwards education had to adopt a more utilitarian and instrumental culture, where 'fitness for purpose' is underpinned by control and an ideology of learning targets. As a result teachers have themselves frequently come to regard in-service training and advanced study in instrumental terms. A 'tips for teachers' approach has been fostered, where the consideration of wider issues relating to disadvantage, social control and ideology have been at best peripheral to the need to provide Year 7 with something decent to do after break tomorrow.

An attempt to gather reliable information concerning societal influences on special education is fraught with considerable difficulty, not least because of the charge of environmental determinism and a so-called deficit interpretation of the lives of students who have special educational needs. As a result there is evidence that the protagonists for a 'macro-environmental effect' lobby have retired, or at least semi-retired, to their ideological shell. Nowhere is this more noticeable than in teacher education, where students who have been schooled exclusively during a period when right-wing political ideology has been ascendant, have increasingly adopted an instrumentalist view of their role as new teachers. Whilst this is regrettable there are some rays of hope on the horizon, notably as a result of the developments that have taken place in micro-sociology. I will consider these in the next section of this chapter.

Prior to that, however, it is worth acknowledging the work of sociologists in providing an explanation for the correlation between social and economic background and problem behaviour in schools. As I have indicated earlier, there is a long tradition of work which illustrates this link, and a number of studies can be used as illustrations (Douglas, 1964; Kellmer-Pringle, Butler and Davie, 1966). In more detail, the Newsom Report (1963) concluded that problems of indiscipline were largely concentrated in 'problem areas'. These, according to the report, were 'areas of bad housing with a high concentration of social problems'. Schostak (1983) referred to the urban focus of deviant behaviour in classrooms, suggesting that the high school in Slumptown used in his study was 'typical of the social and historical process which has produced other slump towns throughout Great Britain'. Mortimore and Blackstone (1982) acknowledged the persistent negative relationship between social disadvantage and educational attainment.

Each of these studies represents a continuation of a tradition in the literature which sought to expose the lack of opportunity which prevailed in the education system and which was most felt by those school students who had special educational needs. Sociologists have been influential in developing theories as to why this should be the case. Examples of this may be drawn from the exemplary work of Bowles and Gintis (1976) in the USA and Tomlinson (1982). The argument that I have made is that, whilst such theories appear to be sound in rationale, they have come to be regarded as rhetorical outpourings of the disenfranchised left-wing, at a time when political and educational ideology has shifted its base to encompass a dogmatic insistence on self-help, the reascendance of single-subject teaching, of control and discipline and of prescription in both curriculum and organization of learning. One of the considerable battles that we face, therefore, is to reinforce the link between education and society: this may best be done by a focus on the micro–macro paradigm.

Traditional interpretations of the correlation between educational attainment and social disadvantage have been criticized because they suggested a deterministic view of the role of the school student who has special educational needs. Typical of this criticism was the view of Furlong (1985), who argued that the sociologist operating within a positivistic paradigm views the world as being 'made up of social facts which are "real" and external to the individual'. The views of the social actors are not considered and their actions, meanings and feelings are regarded as irrelevant.

The period from about 1970 onwards saw a dramatic shift in thinking in the sociology of education. This, it may be argued, was in part a reaction to such environmental determinism. As a result, considerable focus began to be placed upon individual schools and on the role of the school students within them. This is the subject of the next part of this chapter.

Micro-sociology and schools

Ball (1981) summarized the then preoccupation of sociologists of education with the macro-theoretical issues of socio-economic class, gender and race. He commented that 'It is virtually impossible to find sociological accounts that employ the words and meanings of the educated themselves as sources of data.' This situation, he argued, resulted in what Stenhouse (1979) regarded as the predictive social science model, in which case-study approaches using the teacher as a participant and the views of 'the educated themselves' were regarded to be far less important than analyses of regional or national policy.

The work of Bronfenbrenner (1979) is of considerable importance in this respect. The underpinning theme of his work on ecosystems (see also Chapter 11, p. 149) was that any understanding of human development should not be limited to an investigation of a single setting. It should take account of 'aspects of the environment beyond the immediate situation containing the subject'. The challenge, therefore, was to use the 'narrow visions of behaviour and development' (Apter, 1982) to draw a set of wider conclusions about the structural features of society which influenced the (inappropriate) behaviour in the first place.

Partly as a result of this challenge, the 'new' sociology of the 1970s onwards began to adopt a more individualized approach, in which the importance of individual schools and the views of both teachers and school students were recognized. Many teachers will be familiar with the seminal studies within this new paradigm: Willis (1977), Woods (1979), Rutter *et al.* (1979), Everhart (1983) and Woods (1990) all chart the progress towards a sophisticated approach to sociological inquiry within small-scale settings.

The success of this alternative approach may have been possible because of a number of factors. The political, economic and social uncertainties which have preoccupied society in the 1970s and 1980s, and which have impacted on education systems, have meant that teachers began to turn inwards, to look at issues within their own schools and professional practices. It may be that teachers felt that, by doing this, they had at least some degree of control over certain aspects of their work at a time when hegemony increasingly prevailed in educational decision-making during the 1980s.

An ideological shift in special education, from the period around the Warnock Report (1978), could also explain in part this micro-focus. Although political rhetoric still abounded in the resulting Education Act 1981, there was some evidence that those students who were considered to have special educational needs were being viewed in a more equable way than hitherto. Additionally, teachers working in schools began to feel that, as a result of classroom-based research, sociologists were at last beginning to address the problems that they faced on a day-to-day basis. Finally, the academic status of small-scale sociological inquiry was increased, following the success of many researchers adopting case-study methodology in making theoretical, macro-generalizations from their work.

A recent study (Garner, 1993) can be used to illustrate this approach, and the way in which practical outcomes for teachers and students in schools can result from small-scale research which sought to highlight differences between the reality of these participants and the rhetoric of the school as an institution. A synopsis of this study forms the second part of this section.

Amongst that group of school students with special educational needs, those who are termed disruptive are possibly the most marginalized. Theirs is a non-normative and informal category, in which subjective definition has remained a problem. Moreover, they are often viewed with far less sympathy by adults than are those students who have physical disability or who experience learning difficulty. Thus Howard and Lloyd-Smith (1990) argued that society would attempt to justify inadequate segregated provision for 'disruptive' students on the grounds that such students are themselves responsible for their own behaviour and failure to learn (see Chapter 1, p. 3). Theirs is, incontrovertibly, that 'condition' which has traditionally been regarded as being influenced by individual (or within-student) and environmental (societal) factors.

In this research I chose to investigate the views of two groups of 'disruptive' students in two schools in England and the USA. Whilst the purpose of the work was to compare the views of students between two countries, so that cross-national inferences could be made, the research indicated a number of interesting features within each country concerning the relationship between the disruptive students, their teachers and schools, and contextual factors relating to socio-economic class.

Both schools were located in towns of between 50,000 and 70,000 inhabitants. Both towns had industrial bases which were declining as a result of recession in their country's national economy in the late 1980s. The schools in which the investigation took place served catchment areas which were socially and economically mixed: this view was based upon four factors: the percentage of households possessing a car, the percentage of economically active residents, the percentage of households which were not owner-occupiers and the percentage of households with more than one person per room. The two schools in the study were high schools with between 500 and 750 students on roll, and catered for the full ability range.

The investigation, in which statements were gathered from twelve male students in each school, who were regarded as disruptive by their teachers, suggested that whilst many negative views were expressed concerning school, a significant minority of views indicated that the students held positive opinions about their lives at school. Thus, in each of the four aspects of school life investigated (the curriculum, the teachers, problem behaviour and school organization) the students' views were by no means wholly oppositional to the normative values of their school. This appears to contradict the macro-view that so-called disruptive students operate within a subcultural model, where conflict by means of resistance is a structural feature of their response to formal education.

Of particular importance in the study was the inference that the personality and professional demeanour of their teachers was an important factor in promoting a positive response from the disruptive students to both individual subjects in the curriculum and to school rules regarding antisocial behaviour. Moreover, there was some correlation between the views of 'disruptive' students and those of other students who were not identified as 'disruptive', and also with the views of the teachers in the two schools. Again, this appears to conflict with accepted wisdom, which has tended to suggest that students who are termed disruptive adopt strategies and beliefs which do not correspond to those of the school community as a whole.

In a series of supporting case studies of individual disruptive students, the research amplified the notion that there was a link between environmental factors and the students' categorization as 'disruptive'. By using school records from both their primary and secondary schools it became apparent that, in most cases, the students were drawn from families which experienced a high level of stress caused by the factors to which Castle (1958) referred. Moreover, in each case the students were drawn from communities which experienced considerable social and economic deprivation, as indicated by the indices of disadvantage mentioned earlier.

The assumption from this was that, whilst the two schools catered for students from a wide range of social backgrounds, the disruptive students in the study were almost exclusively linked to disadvantaged environments within the catchment. A recognition of that fact, exemplified in one small-scale research, may be helpful in drawing substantive macro-conclusions concerning the 'roots, careers and prospects' (West, 1982) of the disruptive student in schools and, in particular, the ways in which schools and education systems might change in order to incorporate this group of students more effectively in the education process.

Certainly, in the case study described it was apparent that the teachers in the two locations were at least acknowledging the fact that educational disadvantage was, to a great extent, linked to the social backgrounds of particular students. This, in turn, was helping to inform their professional practices in relation to the disruptive students in their schools. The potential, for schools in general, of developments in such approaches is explored in the concluding part of this chapter.

Using micro-sociology to change schools

It is apparent, from much of the existing literature concerning disruptive students, that their views have formed, until relatively recently, only a minor contribution to the debate concerning the management of these students in schools. The Elton Report (DES, 1989c), for example, did not seek to establish the views of students concerning problem behaviour in its inquiry into discipline in schools: conversely, the opinions of teachers formed a substantive and detailed part of the research which supported the report.

As a result of a developing interest in micro-sociology, outlined earlier in this chapter, there has been some evidence that sociologists have been instrumental in developing a recent tradition of researching the views of students in schools. Amongst this work are a number of notable examples of studies which have sought to use the views of disruptive students to make innovations concerning school organization and professional practice. In this way, it has been argued, teachers may subsequently be more able to recognize that, for disruptive students, school processes are often a reflection of the marginalized position which they occupy within society: micro and macro can thus be subsumed in a rational ideology which supports the incorporation of disruptive students into the professional practices of teachers themselves.

This strategy has been particularly evident in the USA. There, the work of Stallworth, Frechtling and Frankel (1983), Murtaugh and Zeitlin (1989), Furtwengler (1990) and Stevenson (1991) has provided good examples of the use that can be made of the views of disruptive students to significantly alter management practice in the school, so that it is made more responsive to the aspirations and feelings, often culturally framed, of this group of students.

Stevenson illustrates this rationale by arguing that the managerial perspective, which is based upon the normative ideology of control, tends to view disruptive students as detrimental to the quality of classroom life. What he refers to as the 'collective resource perspective', on the other hand, allows the development and enforcement of rules and procedures through a process of negotiation, which involves the students themselves as agencies rather than fixed, structural components. This kind of thinking had already begun to gather some momentum in England (McKelvey and Kyriacou, 1985).

Whilst there are considerable professional doubts about the efficacy of this approach to student advocacy, particularly when it involves disruptive students, there is equally a growing acknowledgement that this strategy can represent a significant step towards a recognition that, whilst disruptive students may well be products of disadvantage, they are by no means wholly alienated from the schooling process. This, in turn, may be a useful point from which changes in school organization can take place. If it can be demonstrated to the significant adults in schools that even the disruptive students place considerable importance on what may be regarded as the 'traditional' values of hard work and respect for others then it may well be that an ideological understanding between staff and students can be forged.

Hitherto, in the sociology of special education, much has been written concerning the differences that exist between what the disruptive students actually experience (their reality) and the alternative interpretations of those experiences by teachers and administrators (the rhetoric). Carrier (1989) provides one example of the way in which this approach has been commonplace in special education. Small-scale, school-based inquiries, of the type outlined earlier in this chapter, also help to demonstrate that such differences, between rhetoric and reality, may be counterproductive to the effective management of the education of disruptive students.

Thus, both schools in the cited study claimed a student-centred orientation, in which the written aims included statements that they provided 'enhanced opportunities for those students who are the victims (*sic*) of social and economic disadvantage' and that they would 'discriminate positively in favour of disadvantaged groups' (Garner, 1993). The views of the students (and the teachers) in the two schools indicate an alternative reality. The former show in many of their statements that, rather than being supported, they feel marginalized within the school community. As one student said to me, 'teachers here make the rules and then they say, "We're all in this together"'. The teachers' comments gave supporting evidence to the reality gap which existed between what actually happened to the students and their own perception of events. The view of one teacher, in the English school, was that 'we have a well-developed and caring pastoral system'. It is doubtful if this understanding is shared by the disruptive students.

In this chapter I have tried to re-present the notion that, by taking more account of what goes on within the school, in particular the social interactions between the participants, important links can be re-established between school and society. This relationship, I have argued, has become increasingly fractured as we have moved towards a far more instrumentalist educational culture. A micro-sociological approach confirms the importance of what Bronfenbrenner referred to as the microsystem, the one-to-one relationship of teacher and student, within a much larger social structure. A classroom-based approach, therefore, may well be a point of entry, or re-entry, into a sociology of education which is not seen as fixed or deterministic, and yet emphasizes that there is a continuum between societal disadvantage and access to quality education. The reinforcement of this linkage remains fundamental to progress.

For the reader
Try, at least once every term, to discuss with your own pupils or students, their own perceptions and priorities within school. If this is undertaken regularly and seriously, it will quickly advance beyond sycophancy, self-indulgence and/or triviality.

9

A Special Special Need: Self-Advocacy, Curriculum and the Needs of Children with Severe Learning Difficulties

Viv Hinchcliffe

In this chapter I will present and discuss the psychological roots of self-advocacy, namely a person's developing social cognitive awareness. Secondly, I will look at the mismatch between a developmental curriculum and the National Curriculum and the way that the latter may have distracted teachers' attention away from focusing upon individual needs. Finally, I will outline some areas of work which may help children with severe learning difficulties express their desires, beliefs and intentions.

Self-advocacy is about making our own decisions, demanding our own entitlements and asserting our rights (Clements, 1987). Clearly, our ability to self-advocate relies upon our cognitive and linguistic skills. Traditionally, people with severe learning difficulties, who generally have developmental delay in these areas, are viewed as having poor self-management skills and are seen as a group of people who need others to advocate on their behalf. For some individuals, for example people with profound and multiple difficulties, self-advocacy may be seen as an unrealistic aim, and people will need to advocate on their behalf for the duration of their lives.

Self-advocacy is one of the ways that we actively direct our own destiny; it is a means by which we make our desires, beliefs and intentions known, usually to people who have some control over us. We learn much about this during childhood. Toddlers in the 'terrible twos' are constantly learning how best they can get their own way, learning a great deal about themselves and their care-givers at the same time. They learn how and whom they can manipulate. In order to state a case, a person must have a degree of personal and social understanding. One has to be able to make decisions, analyse problems and be able to select an action which might resolve the problem (Clements, 1987). Self-advocacy stems from our powers of self-control. It is to do with self-awareness, the process by which we come to understand ourselves – our appraisal of our limitations, strengths and weaknesses. Before we can speak up for what we want, we have to learn about ourselves, learn about what we lack, what we need and what it is feasible to expect. This type of knowledge about the self and others is called social cognition. A person's powers of self-advocacy are seen to be reliant upon social cognitive skills, and development in this area is regarded as a major catalyst for empowerment.

You will not find reference to social cognition or self-advocacy in the National Curriculum Programmes of Study (PoS) and Attainment Targets (ATs), the reason being, as we shall see, that non-intellectually disabled children develop self-awareness incidentally, through ordinary daily life and social experience. But for the child with severe learning difficulties, such incidental learning about the self cannot be taken for granted; it often needs to be fostered and taught. Children at early development levels, for example children with profound learning disability, may have only a rudimentary understanding of the self and other. However, raised teachers' expectations for these students, particularly in respect of looking for communicative signals and offering opportunities for choice and decision-making, is seen as a major route to empowerment for these students. An infant's ability to communicate intentionally in the first year of life demonstrates an awareness of another person's intentions (Bates, Camaioni and Volterra, 1975; Camaioni, 1992). The development of intentional communication in the person with profound learning difficulties shows that he has an awareness that someone is likely to act upon his communication; that there is some understanding of the self/ other distinction.

Some people with a learning disability have a particular difficulty in their development of personal and social cognition. Several studies have indicated that children with autism have a specific developmental delay in appreciating another person's point of view, particularly the mental states of others (Baron-Cohen, Leslie and Frith, 1985; Perner *et al.*, 1989). A feature of autism is impaired interpersonal skills (Wing, 1981). Clearly this will affect the person's ability to state a case, for unless someone has an appreciation of another person's point of view, then he will not make a case in such a way that it is acceptable and convincing to that other person.

It is not just developmental delay that militates against the person's ability to self-advocate. A person's attempts to achieve change by her own efforts depend upon whether these actions are going to be valued by people in control. Empowerment through effectively stating one's case rather depends upon whether one's intentions are heard. Winchurst, Kroese and Adams (1992) talk about the environmental factors that inhibit self-advocacy: 'a person's lack of exposure to "real-life" social interaction, differential (often patronising) treatment from others, and therefore infrequent opportunities to make and express real choices'. Clements (1987) talks about the need for modified expectations about people with severe learning disabilities, viewing them as 'people with a potential for self-efficacy, rather than as being forever passive and dependent, requiring a high degree of external control'.

Interest in giving pupils with severe learning difficulties an increased role to play in their own learning came in the middle 1980s when teachers became interested in process-content models of teaching and learning. In this model, more emphasis was placed upon negotiation, problem-solving, mutual understanding and self-development (Smith, 1987, 1991). Teachers became critical of behavioural approaches, which were seen to be too prescriptive and leading to stereotypical learning with limited opportunities for generalization. Since 1970, when children with severe learning difficulties were officially admitted into the education system, behavioural-product approaches dominated teaching and learning in special education. Here, the teacher was concerned with observable behaviour, behaviour which could be measured. Specific objectives were devised so that mastery could be determined within given criteria for success. Teachers used task analysis to break down behavioural objectives into manageable steps. Even some higher-order mental processes, including language, were subjected to a behavioural methodology (see Leeming et al., 1979). In the 1980s interest was shown in interactive-process approaches to teaching. Teachers who found security in the masses of teacher-prescribed behavioural objectives, ticks and prompt codes were now being to encouraged to let their children take the lead and pay more attention to the process of teaching and learning. There was more interest in the development of process skills which generalized across the demands of other learning situations (Ashman and Conway, 1989). Teachers began to examine children's behaviour in the contexts in which they found themselves. Much more emphasis was placed on the learning environment, providing opportunities for problem-solving, choice making and peer interaction (Goldbart, 1988). This model has close parallels to Schon's (1983) 'professional artistry' model, where professional activity is seen as a practical art. Understanding is stressed in preference to technical skills, improvisation is recognized and teachers view knowledge as temporary, dynamic and problematic rather than absolute and permanent (Fish, 1991). Schon's professional artistry model has great application to the education of children with severe learning difficulties. For much of the work is unpredictable; the children are unpredictable. Teachers are continually coping with the unexpected and often find themselves thinking on their feet, improvising and reading the situation, what Schon calls 'reflection in action.' The complex nature of the child's learning difficulties forces the teacher to focus upon individual need and 'reflect in action'. The teacher may be clear about where she is going, but she often has to change direction to get there.

In terms of language and communication, much less emphasis was placed upon children's competence within grammarian language programmes. Teachers of children at early stages of development were becoming less interested in teaching language performance within stimulus-response procedures, for example in object labelling. Teachers were less preoccupied with achieving a match between teacher language and child language. More interest was shown in pragmatics – the functions of language – observing what children can do with their existing communication, how they make demands on their environment and the people within it. From the interactive-process approaches to teaching and learning, the teacher's stance was more respectful of the child's current level of performance. Expectations were perhaps raised, children were not seen to require as much external control. Closer observation of the way children were functionally communicating meant that teachers were less likely to anticipate need; a sure way of disempowering the individual. In a climate of greater interaction, children were seen less as passive recipients and more as active learners, with perhaps greater opportunity to express their own needs and interests. More and more the teacher's behaviour was guided by that of the child.

If self-advocacy is seen on a continuum of self-expression then the ability to choose according to known preferences may be seen as an important developmental milestone. Houghton, Bronicki and Guess (1987) found that staff working with students with severe disabilities responded at very low rates to student-initiated opportunities of choice or preference. The authors of this study state that their research supports previous observations that the 'education of students with severe disabilities is dominated by stimulus control techniques and instructional procedures. Possibly, this heavy emphasis distracts from both observing and responding to student-initiated behaviour, including expressions of choice and preference.' Houghton *et al.* see the responsiveness of attending adults to expressions of preference as crucial to the early development of communication skills in that it fosters a reciprocal relationship between child and care-giver. They suggest that teachers have not been trained to observe and respond to 'subtle but potentially valuable nuances of behaviour that reflect attempts by the students to express themselves, especially among those students with severe motor and sensory impairments'.

Judith Coupe's work does much to address this issue. *The Affective Communication Assessment* (Coupe *et al.*, 1985) provides the structure by which teachers working with children at preintentional levels of communication can interpret their affective responses to various stimuli and place meaning on them; to respond to them as if they are communicative signals. Affective responses include expressions of like, dislike, want and reject. Coupe's work on 'affective communication' was based on the way mothers and fathers attach meaning to early infant behaviours (Coupe *et al*., 1985; Coupe and Goldbart, 1988). This work looked closely at how the infant's efforts to act on her environment became signals to the mother who then assigns to them communicative intent. Reciprocity develops, that is the infant learns to attend to the care-giver's language and actions and begins to respond during appropriate pauses. Research into mother–infant interaction has shown the young infant's ability to initiate and terminate interactions with her care-giver through body movement, facial expression, eye contact and vocalization (Stern, 1977; Trevarthen, 1977). More recent research has demonstrated the remarkable abilities of the infant in the first few weeks of life (Meltzoff and Moore, 1983; Glenn and Cunningham, 1984; Glenn, 1987). The research into mother–infant interaction has helped to raise teachers' expectations of the potential of pupils at early developmental levels. It has certainly led to a great deal of curriculum innovation. Hewett and Nind's approach to 'intensive interaction' draws upon the natural responsiveness of parents to their young infants. In this approach to working with people at early stages of development, Hewett and Nind let the disabled person take the lead, centring upon 'dialogues' of imitation, rhythm, repetition and expectancy (Hewett and Nind, 1992).

And then came the National Curriculum, the epitome of prescriptive teaching. The implementation of the National Curriculum in schools for children with severe learning difficulties has militated against curriculum innovation and has redirected teachers' attention away from a number of exciting and innovative new approaches to teaching and learning. It is ironic that in popular talk about children's 'entitlement' to a universal 'broad and balanced' curriculum, we are losing sight of important 'narrow and specific' curricular areas for pupils with severe learning difficulties. One such area is developing children's social cognition. We read time and time again that the National Curriculum is only part of the whole school curriculum and that schools are free to continue working with tried and tested principles of good practice and experiment with new principles of teaching and learning. In theory, this is true; in practice, it is unlikely. Since the Education Reform Act 1988, teachers have had very little time to reflect upon their practice. Their attention has been deflected from looking at children's individual needs to trying to implement a centrally imposed common curriculum. I see this as representing a move away from child-centred education. I consider a subject-led curriculum to be foreign to the tried and tested formula for good practice in special education: to observe, to assess, to develop teaching programmes according to individual need and then to evaluate. This is, of course, what teachers are still doing, but the job is made more difficult when teachers have to demonstrate (or perhaps in reality pay lip service to) the National Curriculum. Teachers in special schools are still interested in curriculum innovation. However, there would be more evidence of it if teachers were not preoccupied with grappling with the National Curriculum.

Even the journals are engrossed with National Curriculum. A search through recent editions of the *British Journal of Special Education* shows a plethora of reports, articles and commentaries about National Curriculum. Anyone would think that it was devised with the child with special needs in mind. Only the research section seems spared of National Curriculum, and I see this as significant. This is because, in the main, this is where work actually centres upon the specific learning needs of children with learning difficulties (for example, Porter's (1993) excellent discussion about children's understanding of counting). What distinguishes these articles from the rest is that the research is directed at trying to understand the difficulties that children with severe learning difficulties experience in their learning. This work can be considered child centred if it helps teachers target areas of learning difficulty. Teachers need to read more research articles of this type, work that identifies where children may fail to learn, in order that teachers can examine their own practice with a view to refining and improving it. Research should feed curriculum innovation.

The National Curriculum was seen as a curriculum for all (NCC, 1989); the Education Reform Act 1988 promoted the spirit of 'entitlement'. The needs of children with severe learning difficulties were clearly not at the forefront of anyone's mind when the National Curriculum was devised, piloted and gradually introduced into mainstream schools. Special schools were given a year of grace, to consider ways of incorporating the initiatives into special school practice. How much easier it would have been if the DES had been more honest about its lack of understanding of the educational needs of the child with severe learning difficulties. How much easier it would have been if during 1989 representatives from the DES had consulted teachers from special education and looked at the feasibility of testing and the relevance of ATs for children at early stages of development. If the education of children with severe learning difficulties was higher up the agenda of DES interest, this consultation may have taken place, and National Curriculum may have had different status in SLD schools; it may have been more flexible, more child centred and, most importantly, it may have been more optional. How much more sensible it would have been to leave it to the schools and parents of children with severe learning difficulties (who know the children best) to select the best from the National Curriculum. This would have encouraged teachers to look at the breadth of their existing curricula (and in 1988 there were a number of schools which did not have a written curriculum). Schools could then supplement their development curricula with relevant National Curriculum PoS. This would have gone a long way to promote positive curriculum innovation and the raising of teachers' expectations. Instead, in mainstream and special education, the way that the DES has gone about its policy of education reform has provoked resistance to testing and league tables, and many would say that the government's intentions to raise standards have been misguided. The consequences of not initially considering the needs of children with severe learning difficulties before implementing universal reform or, worse, not seeking the advice of people who know about the needs of these children is that teachers in special schools are now spending massive amounts of time struggling to implement the National Curriculum.

At the time of writing, there seems to be a slow about-turn in thinking about the relevance of the National Curriculum to children with severe learning difficulties at early developmental levels. Ware (1990) writes about fighting for the right of every child to receive a curriculum which is individually tailored to his or her own individual needs. She accepts that for many children with severe learning difficulties (SLD) this curriculum should include the National Curriculum but wonders about the appropriateness and benefit to children with profound and multiple learning difficulties. The National Curriculum Council (NCC, 1992) stated that when the National Curriculum was being formulated 'it was impossible to legislate for the enormous diversity of special educational needs'. Hinchcliffe and the MSD1 course team (1992), in their review of this document, believed this statement to be both 'a simplification and a cop-out'. They question whether the principle of 'entitlement' has been taken on board by most SLD schools and note how this principle has been treated with reverence in the literature published in the wake of the Education Reform Act 1988.

In *Special Needs in the National Curriculum: Opportunity and Challenge*, published in March 1993, the National Curriculum Council, perhaps for the first time, has addressed teachers' concerns about the difficulties of including children with 'exceptionally severe learning difficulties' in National Curriculum initiatives. Teachers of these children reported that 'meeting individual objectives of a developmental or a self-help nature must remain central to the curriculum for these pupils'. The review states, 'although progression for these pupils cannot be traced through levels in the National Curriculum attainment targets, planning from PoS does enable pupils to progress in small stages and that progress can be monitored and recognised' (NCC, 1993).

Despite these encouraging signs, it seems that there are only a few people, in print anyway, who are prepared to challenge and debate the relevance of the National Curriculum to the education of children with severe learning difficulties. It is time now to turn to more child-centred issues.

Social cognition and self-advocacy

Social cognition primarily concerns our understanding of the people in our world. Flavell (1985) writes that social cognition 'means cognition about people and their doings'. Earlier in his writings, Flavell *et al.* (1977) state that it includes 'perception, thinking and knowledge regarding the self, other people, social relations, social organization and institutions – in general, our human, social world'. Staff of Rectory Paddock School (1983) prefer to call social cognition 'personal–social cognition' to emphasize the importance of knowledge of the self as well as other people. A person's powers of self-advocacy are dependent upon her social cognitive development. In order to state her case and act purposefully upon choice-making opportunities, a person must have an understanding of the self. Self-advocates must have an understanding of themselves, in the sense that they must know what they want. They should also know their own limitations and be realistic about their intentions. Self-advocates making their case to another person (usually to a person who has greater control) should ideally have an understanding of the other person's point of view; for if they are to persuade someone of their case, then their case will be strengthened if they do so in a way that is considered reasonable, feasible and rational. The development of social cognition in pupils with severe learning difficulties is an important prerequisite to their powers of self-advocacy.

Hinchcliffe and Roberts (1987) state that in attempting to improve children's development of social cognition, teachers are faced with the problem that this type of cognition deals with intangible entities, which cannot be directly perceived or demonstrated – 'thoughts, feelings, wishes, intentions, attitudes, knowledge, memory, motivation, comprehension, etc.' However, the authors add that there is one helpful factor, that most pupils with severe learning difficulties can be assumed to have experienced these things within themselves, at least in some rudimentary form. They write:

> They feel emotions, they remember people and places, they are motivated to achieve certain purposes, they understand certain things, and so on. Our aim in developing social cognition is to make the children consciously aware of all these mental events and activities, both within themselves and, by analogy, within other people.

(Hinchcliffe and Roberts, 1987, p. 77)

Language clearly plays a key part in social cognition and self-advocacy, particularly language that refers to intentions, desires and beliefs. Hinchcliffe and Roberts analysed parental reports of the spontaneous language of a group of Down's syndrome children aged between two and eleven years. The authors found a paucity of mental state language being used by the sample. Preliminary findings from the authors' follow-up study investigating the frequency and type of internal state language among children with severe learning difficulties has shown a similar poverty of internal state language. Internal state language is words which refer to people's intentions, cognitions and feeling states. Clearly the ability to share information about the above plays an important part in self-advocacy. Hinchcliffe and Roberts found certain teaching strategies to be effective in teaching 'target' words which were used to develop conscious awareness of mental events and feelings, as well as the ability to talk about them (see Hinchcliffe and Roberts (1987) for a fuller discussion). The categories and lists of target words are reproduced in the Table.

Vocabulary of target words about mental and personal properties

(A) **Character/behaviour language:** careful, careless, kind, unkind, generous, mean, polite, rude, friendly, gentle, lazy, helpful, greedy, patient, honest, cheerful, cruel, responsible, stubborn, thoughtful

(B) **Attitude/emotion language:** happy, pleased, glad, sad, unhappy, grateful, angry, cross, frightened, afraid, scared, worried, hope, look forward to, disappointed, excited, bored, sorry, ashamed, jealous, wish, proud, shy, embarrassed, lonely, fed up

(C) **Perception language:** see, hear, smell, feel (physically), notice

(D) **Metacognitive language:** know, think, remember, forget, mean (intend), wish, hope, wonder, guess (English), believe, understand, be sure, expect, find out, idea, decide, make up mind, change mind

(E) **Truth value/reality language:** right (a statement), true (a statement), wrong (a statement), pretend, mistake, dream, trick, joke, act, mean (speaker), story, really happen, not really happen

(F) **Metalinguistic language (incl speech acts):** understand, mean (words), explain, argue, pretend, lie, ask, agree, promise, apologise, tell off, cheer up, remind, thank, persuade

---

From Hinchcliffe, V. and Roberts, M. (1987) Developing social cognition and Metacognition, in B. Smith (ed.) *Interactive Approaches to the Education of Children with Severe Learning Difficulties*, Westhill College, Birmingham.

Sections (A) and (B) are self-explanatory. In terms of self-advocacy, the ability of people with severe learning disability to use character/behaviour language and talk about their own emotional state using some of the words listed may be seen as extremely important to a group of people who may be exploited, vulnerable, or overprotected. I feel this becomes increasingly important when students reach adolescence and start to make relationships. The words listed under section (C) – Perception language – were included because our work revealed how difficult many of our students found it to verbalize about perceptual experience. The metacognitive words listed in section (D) refer to states of knowledge or awareness (or the lack of them, for example 'I forget', 'I don't know', 'I don't understand', etc.). Clearly, the person who can reflect upon his own knowledge state or awareness, is in a far better position to reason about his own desires, beliefs and intentions.

Section (E) – Truth value/reality language – is an important category because so many of our pupils find it difficult to 'take communications as cognitive objects and critically analyze them' (Flavell, 1981). Our ability to offer judgements about statements comes so easily to us in everyday speech that it is easy to overlook how difficult this is for many students with severe learning difficulty. Included under this heading are words relating to knowledge of the distinction between appearance and reality. The acquisition of such knowledge is, according to Flavell, Speer and Green (1983),

> a very important developmental problem . . . . The distinction arises in a very large number and variety of ecologically significant cognitive situations. In many of these situations, the information available to us is insufficient or misleading, causing us to accept an apparent state of affairs (appearance) that differs from the true state of affairs (reality).
>
> (Flavell *et al.*, 1983, p. 99)

For the reasons stated above, relating to possible exploitation and deception, we must help our pupils to become more aware of this difference and to verbalize their judgements about it. Finally, under (F) – Metalinguistic language – we list words about language and some of its functions. Awareness of the ways in which people use language to get what they want plays an important role in self-advocacy. Cazden defines metalinguistic knowledge or awareness as 'the ability to make language forms opaque and attend to them in and for themselves' (Cazden, 1983 p. 103). When expressing self-interests, a person's ability to give reasons for her judgements when faced with a counter-argument is an important consideration when defending a case. Hinchcliffe and Roberts offer suggestions about teaching strategies to help students to give reasons for their judgements.

Teaching the meaning of such words with the aim that the children will be able to use them is seen as a valuable means of empowering students to talk about intentions, cognitions and feeling states. Personal experience of teaching pupils with severe learning difficulties over a number of years has demonstrated that spontaneous usage of many of these words is limited. Teaching children the meaning of social cognitive terms through story-telling and short plays has been successful in encouraging children to label some of their feelings and intentions, an area of the curriculum that I feel should be given greater emphasis. The value of encouraging children to express feeling states need not be spelt out. Regular opportunities to discuss the meaning of internal states in small groups occasionally elicits some interesting insights into the children's thinking. Although this work has shown the considerable difficulties that children with severe learning difficulties experience in understanding or producing a definition of a word, children can, by degrees, grasp the meaning of some highly abstract terms. In recent discussion with a group of pupils, we were talking about 'jealousy'. Here, we were talking about the latest events in a popular television soap. These provide some rich material for talking about internal states. In another session, one student spontaneously provided a rare example of a definition of a targeted word, saying that 'disappointment means when you want something to happen and it doesn't happen'.

This brings us on to a potentially difficult area for teachers when working on the meanings of some of the words in the Table. This concerns the child's realization that she has a learning disability or an awareness that certain aspects of her life are not under her complete control. In my teaching experience, student references to this level of self-awareness are fairly rare, due to the level of social cognitive development (or more specifically, metacognitive awareness) necessary for this type of self-appraisal. However, when attention is drawn to this by the student (and within intervention based upon social cognition and metacognition, perhaps, it is more likely to happen) then I feel the teacher must answer questions honestly and sensitively. After all, in terms of self-advocacy, the more realistic a person's self-appraisal is, the more realistic her expectations are likely to be.[1] It is distressing to talk to students who have very unrealistic expectations about life beyond school, in terms of work, relationships, independence, etc.

This chapter has attempted to show that social cognition is the foundation for children's developing skills in self-advocacy. Children's success or failure in their ability to express their desires, beliefs and intentions depends largely on how far we can make them aware of their own cognitive processes. Self-advocacy depends upon self-awareness, but it also relies upon knowledge and understanding of the desires, beliefs and intentions of other people.

Tensions between a developmental curriculum and the National Curriculum come to light when we examine the specific learning needs of certain groups of children. In the last five years it has become less fashionable to dwell upon individual need. This is very apparent when one considers current legislation. I look forward to the return to a needs-driven education system.

Note
(1) The reader is invited to refer back to the section on individual psychotherapy (p. 60) (ed.).

For the reader
Consider the ability of your own pupils or students (with or without learning difficulties) to express fluently their emotions and needs. How much are you doing to move them beyond simplistic descriptors like 'boring' or 'wicked'?

Introduction to Chapter 10

People who have been working in special education for some time often forget their introduction to the subject. Sometimes our first encounter is as the result of some personal contact, sometimes people enter special education almost by accident. In any case the initial sharpness of our perceptions becomes dulled, sometimes we even cease to see the differences ourselves. The next chapter describes the experiences of some very surprised student teachers and gives us pause for thought about how we induct new teachers into special education. In the new subject-oriented and overcrowded teacher education course, cross-curricular issues must be 'permeated', introduced in the course of the attention given to the subject specialism. Is this the best way to raise the awareness of student teachers about the wide range of human ability and experience which awaits them?

10

Oh my God, Help!: What Newly Qualifying Teachers Think of Special Schools

Philip Garner

I recall a few years ago a friend who worked in a school for children with severe learning difficulties (SLD) saying to me that she believed that teachers who work mainly in ordinary schools often have a view that what goes on in special schools is bounded by mystery, medicine and madness. I have also a recent recollection of a colleague, who had a background of teaching similar children, stating that 'all anybody thought I did was "watch the children".'

Whilst the above comments may be regarded as overstatements, there can be little doubt that, for many teachers who work in mainstream schools, what actually happens in special schools remains a secret process, governed by a series of alternative procedures and approaches. These beliefs don't, however, confirm in the minds of these teachers a 'distinctive charm of the small special school' but rather tend to serve merely to compound a stereotype which sees 'difference' as negative. As a consequence, whilst there has been much rhetorical talk of 'making the ordinary school special' or the 'special school ordinary' the assumptions that a lot of teachers have about separate provision remain a major factor in inhibiting a more complete understanding of the issues relating to integration and segregation.

The above commentary is particularly apt in relation to special schools which endeavour to meet the varied educational needs of those children who have SLD. There have, of course, been frequent references in the educational literature to the ways in which teachers build up a predetermined view of the characteristics, personality and learning capabilities of certain groups of children. As a tutor who contributes to a discrete special educational needs element of a one-year teacher training course I thought it would be a useful exercise to attempt to gauge what were the views of newly qualifying teachers concerning SLD schools. It seemed to me that, to some extent, the 'Warnock Wheel' has come to resemble a Catherine wheel: the brightness of the beginning has gradually faded, in the glare of LMS (local management of schools) roman candles and National Curriculum crackerjacks. Students who were about to qualify as teachers would, I felt, provide a litmus test of the extent to which progress has been made towards a more positive and inclusive attitude to special schools in general, and to the children and teachers within them.

Prior to reporting the views of the students it is perhaps worth noting some of the important changes that have taken place in teacher education during the last five years: these have had a material effect not only upon the way in which teachers have been trained for work in primary and secondary schools but also upon the nature of provision for SEN issues within such courses.

The Education Act 1988 marked a landmark in English educational legislation in that, for the first time, a national curriculum (NC) with compulsory core elements became a formative part of instruction in schools (DES, 1989b). It followed that teacher training institutions were required to implement changes in the content of their initial teacher training (ITT) courses, so that important elements of NC organization could be incorporated. This, in turn, meant a diminution of time available for subsidiary subjects and other themes which could be regarded as background issues to a student's general training in education. One such theme has been the issue of SEN.

In 1992 the Department for Education (DfE) published Circular 9/92, which outlined the new criteria and procedures for the initial training of teachers in both primary and secondary phases (DfE, 1992). Fundamental to this document was the belief, outlined in para. 3.4.3, that this training should take place mainly in schools. This, in a similar fashion, meant a shift in emphasis on the part of many higher education (HE) institutions, whereby the increasingly school-based work of ITT courses meant that far less time was available for what may be regarded as cross-curricular, supporting or subsidiary activities. SEN falls into this marginalized category.

One cumulative effect of the training initiatives outlined above has been that those who organize and lecture on teacher training programmes have been forced to adopt a pragmatic approach as to what aspects of the training curriculum should remain. Moreover, the permeation model of SEN work in ITT courses, which has been criticized because it has an 'insufficient foundation by way of specific course content' (DES, 1990b), appears to be the only viable means by which many training institutions can provide even a basic awareness of SEN issues.

Although there is no firm evidence to support the view that a student's exposure to, and understanding of, SEN issues during this new mode of training has been weakened it can be argued that school-based approaches make adequate consideration of SEN something of a lottery: essentially, the level and quality of a student's experience will depend on the school's ability (or willingness) to incorporate SEN as a fundamental aspect of school-based training. This may be even more the case when the spatial location of newly establishing 'training schools' is considered: these may frequently be in catchment areas with a very low occurrence of children who have SEN.

It is against this background of national changes in training ideology and practice that I conducted the present study. It was an attempt to ascertain the views of newly qualifying teachers about special schools (SLD) at the end of a Postgraduate Certificate in Education (PGCE) (Secondary) course in which they had been provided with a compulsory subsidiary course in supportive education, which included elements of both special educational needs (SEN) and personal and social education (PSHE). The main subjects of the student teachers were physical education, geography and religious education.

Two-day visits to eight special schools for children who have severe learning difficulties (SLD) were organized for a full cohort of forty-four student teachers. One school catered for children with 'diverse' learning difficulties: this included a section for pupils with moderate learning difficulties (MLD) and emotional and behavioural difficulties (EBD). The visits took place during the final week of the PGCE course. The student teachers comprised groups of between two and seven, depending on the numbers that each special school felt able to accept. None of the groups received any written instructions concerning the visits, although the student teachers had previously received some training on observation techniques which they had already used in mainstream schools. Additionally, there was a shared understanding, between the student teachers, the teachers and helpers in the school and the college staff that all the students visiting the schools should participate in whatever classroom or other activities were taking place over the two days of the visit: there were to be no bystanders or wallflowers.

The views of the student teachers were assessed subsequent to the visits by means of a six-point questionnaire, focusing upon their reactions to what they had seen and experienced. The questionnaire was completed individually and confidentially by the students at the beginning of a college-based feedback day. Forty-one questionnaires were completed: three students did not attend the feedback day because of job interviews. No discussion with the students prior to their written responses was undertaken. In the analysis of the data which followed no attempt was made to quantify the student responses. Rather, they were used as a means of identifying particular themes and concerns which could form the basis of a subsequent commentary. The opinions of the student teachers concerning their visits were gathered in relation to six points of feedback: each of these will now be considered, and illustrated by the students' verbatim comments, which identify and support particular themes.

The questions
(1) What was your instant reaction on entering the school?

This proved to be a revealing question. The overriding impression gathered from many of the student teachers was one of a personal sense of surprise, shock and uncertainty. Moreover, there was a tension between their perception of the school as an institutionalizing environment and a view which saw the school as a child centred, welcoming place which was a hive of purposeful activity. The latter interpretation became gradually more apparent as the student teachers began to be more relaxed in this new surrounding. The initial reactions, therefore, can best be considered in these two categories.

Many of the student teachers provided frank and honest accounts of their feelings. An overriding sense of anxiety was articulated: 'What is the relevance of anything I am going to do?', 'It was very intimidating . . . what am I doing here . . . am I prepared for this?' and 'Feeling like a member of the cast in *One Flew over the Cuckoo's Nest*: worry and concern at hearing all the noises and seeing the children.' Comments such as these provide ample evidence that little of the work done in either college or in mainstream schools had provided the student teachers with even a basic insight into specialized provision for SLD children. A sense of helplessness and insecurity was summarized by the stark response of one student: 'Oh my God, Help!'

These initial reactions also lend support to the view that many people regard special schools as almost asylum-like institutions. 'As I walked down the drive I thought it was a hospital and not a school . . . the extensive intercom system confirmed my suspicions' and 'I questioned what would these children be capable of learning . . . it seemed like being in a hospital' were comments which characterized the views of several of the student teachers.

These instinctive, shocked and apprehensive responses gradually gave way to a more optimistic and considered view of what was happening in the schools. The student teachers commented with some frequency on the relaxed and friendly environment they experienced: 'A very welcoming school – bright, colourful' and 'It seemed like a hive of activity, staff and pupils everywhere, lots of smiles, a caring (whilst still educational) environment.'

The two categories of responses, outlined above, provide some important pointers to future training approaches in initial teacher training (ITT) courses, which may assist in the process of moving away from the 'mystery, medicine and madness' stereotype. What came as a great surprise to college staff and the teachers in the schools was that, even at the end of a one-year ITT course, in which SEN was a compulsory (and taught) subsidiary component, the student teachers were nevertheless very unprepared for the experience. The students initially expressed great surprise and shock at what they saw, even though most had encountered children who had statements of SEN during their mainstream school experiences. They would, presumably, take these views with them into their mainly mainstream teaching occupations, where it is entirely possible that negative stereotyping might be exacerbated.

Many ITT courses do not provide formal (that is non-permeated) SEN input, and it was agreed by a high proportion of the special school staff participating in this small-scale research that such a situation could only further marginalize special schools, whilst at the same time damaging the prospects of copulative work between them and mainstream schools. Some of the special school staff also commented that this lack of awareness of the work of special schools could potentially damage integration policy.

One student teacher went as far as articulating these concerns as a policy issue for future ITT courses: 'This school would be ideal to visit earlier in the course, and more frequently.' The difficulties of course organization, and in particular time restraints, may tend to militate against such an initiative. Moreover, as all schools become increasingly aware of the financial implications of receiving student teachers on school experience, there would also be a need to ensure that funding, at a realistic level, was made available to special schools to support such an enterprise. Given the existent controversy of funding school-based ITT in mainstream schools this may not be an easy matter to resolve.

Nevertheless, the indication provided in the comments by the student teachers in response to this first question is that experience in special schools may be crucially important in enabling the development of non-stereotypical and informed attitudes towards the work of special schools. It is therefore to be argued that such a process should be encouraged at the outset of a teacher's career, rather than being the product of anecdote and misinformation at a later stage.

(2) How did you feel about meeting the children?

The student teachers again illustrated in their evaluations that initial anxieties and concerns gave way to a more rational and informed view of the children that they encountered in this exercise. Their comments appeared to be equally divided between the student's own reactions and the reactions of the children they met.

Initially, then, there was a feeling of apprehension: would these children *really* be that different? 'Nervous . . . how to approach the children?' 'I felt guilty, sick . . . it was like a different world' and 'I was unsure about how to deal with them. Didn't know if they wanted contact or not' were student comments which summarized this sense of anxiety. The guilt feelings expressed by the student teachers also appeared to be commonplace, and seemed to be borne partly out of their confusion about the role of adults who work with children who have SLD: one student neatly summarized this, stating that she 'felt guilty that I didn't know how to treat them'.

Most of the student teachers indicated that such feelings were transient, however, and that as soon as the initial introductions and contacts had been made they were keen to interact on both a social and educational level. 'After a little while I could let my own feelings subside and relate to them as people' and 'Wary, especially as the first one decided to give me a hug – and he was rather big. Then it was fun to meet all the different children.' As the day progressed this attitude was reinforced, thereby validating the visits as an important means of affirming the children as individuals rather than as 'disabilities': 'At first I didn't know what to expect, but found them particularly friendly – wanting me to be with them all the time. I felt most wanted and rewarded at being able to spend time with them.' Only one student teacher indicated in her comments that the initial anxiety did not ameliorate: 'I was very nervous and apprehensive. These feelings did *not* subside as the day progressed.'

The responses of the student teachers to this question, it has been suggested, were as much about how the children in the school would react to them. An emphasis was, quite naturally, placed upon the perceived communication level of the children, one student providing a synopsis of this concern : 'it took a short while to gauge the severity of the child's communication skills – do they understand? Can they respond verbally?' At the same time the student teachers expressed concerns about the social responses of the children, and several expressed surprise at the proactive nature of the children. One student teacher, for example, commented that 'most of the initiative was taken by them anyway . . . they approached me', a view supported by a further comment that 'They were all very bubbly and interested – not one seemed shy or withdrawn at all.'

(3) How did the character of the school compare with mainstream schools you have visited?

This group of student teacher responses proved to be very illuminating. In one sense it confirmed what many believe to be a fundamental feature of many special schools: the student teachers commented frequently about the distinctive close relationships which existed between staff and pupils, the relaxed yet purposeful atmosphere, and the sense of shared goals. These attributes are worthy of closer examination.

The level of social interaction clearly made an impression on the student teachers, particularly as it was used as the basis for educational activity. One commented that there was a 'Very relaxed atmosphere . . . Each class group had a teacher and a helper but all other staff gave assistance when needed', whilst another remarked that 'The character of the school was totally different. The atmosphere was a happy one and always geared towards the children.' It was also noted that the high level of adult-adult co-operation tended to influence the way in which some of the children worked, with much evidence of 'good pupil-pupil working relationships'. There was, stated one student teacher, 'less of a teacher-pupil divide'.

As the student teachers had recently completed a block teaching practice in mainstream secondary schools they were ideally placed to recognize that the overall ethos of the special schools appeared to be in marked contrast to that of many of the schools they had previously encountered. Special schools, according to one student teacher, 'Seemed to have a very strong school spirit. Many of the teachers/helpers – due to the nature of the work – appeared more like mothers and fathers. Quite a unique atmosphere.' A number of student teachers concluded that the 'feel' of the school seemed to be more like that of a primary school.

This positive interpretation of the ethos of the schools was highlighted in terms of policy matters by several student teachers, and this for them was a major point of difference. 'The school really *did* cater for the special needs of children rather than just print a statement of intent in the school handbook' was a comment which was echoed by four other student teachers in the questionnaires.

A number of differences were highlighted in the organization and staffing of the schools. All of the student teachers made note of the high staff to pupil ratio, whilst time regimentation appeared to be a feature noticeable by its absence: 'It was very different. There is a much more relaxed policy about everything. This is different from mainstream schools where timing is especially regimented.' Everything had the appearance of being 'less rushed and more purposeful, and in some ways more planned and forward thinking'.

There were, none the less, some points of similarity noted. The student teachers, for example, seemed to be quite surprised that both high standards of discipline and a considerable focus on the National Curriculum were very much in evidence. Thus, one suggested that 'It did seem similar: for some reason I didn't expect to see them disciplined and they were. And the National

Curriculum, too.' This similarity was reinforced by others, whose comments were exemplified by the remark that 'Discipline and the reaction by staff to pupils was the same as it would be in mainstream – stern.'

(4) Did anything in particular strike you about the staff?

Responses of student teachers to this question read rather like a thesaurus for a model teacher. First appearances in this respect can be extremely deceptive: 'My first reaction was what a scruffy and strange-looking bunch! But they were really excellent – very patient and treated all the children as if they had no problems.' Almost without exception, in fact, there was a view that the staff they encountered 'all had huge amounts of patience'.

This quality enabled many of the teachers to deal with problems with calmness: 'If something came up they dealt with it quickly, quietly and firmly.' Moreover, the staff in the schools maintained a sense of humour even when placed under stress, so that whilst they appeared 'Very committed to that line of work . . . they always had a sense of fun' and were 'lively and bubbly'.

At the same time the student teachers were impressed by the level of knowledge that the teachers in the special schools showed about individual pupils and the way that this was used to respond to their needs. 'They also knew their pupils inside out' and 'Could tell us everything about the background and stage of development of all of their pupils, like they were reading it from a book.'

Finally, there was an acknowledgement by the student teachers of the level of energy and commitment shown by the teachers, although in one school it was noted that 'They all smoked – was this stress?' But the overriding impression was that the staff in the schools were 'Very strong, both physically and emotionally it seemed.'

(5) What range of SLDs did you encounter?

Comments made by the student teachers in this category revealed a great deal of misunderstanding about the term 'severe learning difficulty'. The definition was frequently confused with others: this did not come as a surprise, since at least three of the student teachers had previously submitted coursework assignments in which they had used the term to denote children who had what were officially categorized as specific learning difficulties. Moreover, it became apparent in their comments that the student teachers tended to focus upon the physical or mental condition of the pupils, rather than upon the learning difficulties which resulted. Where actual learning difficulties were considered they were described in very general terms.

Thus, most student teachers in this study made reference to pupils who had 'physical and mental handicap', 'mentally handicapped . . . and many others undiagnosed: they were just in a world of their own!' and, in one instance, to pupils with 'Down's syndrome and other more serious mental diseases'. One student teacher summarized the range of pupils seen as ranging 'From profound and multiple disorders – kids just about alive, not responding to anything – to mild(?) Down's syndrome kids and some who physically were OK.'

On the other hand, very few of the student teachers made specific reference to actual learning difficulties or capabilities of the children. There was a real sense that the student teachers had difficulty in seeing past the handicapping condition of the pupils, in order to focus upon their educational performances. Nevertheless some reference was made to the fact that 'In one group all had very severe problems in communicating . . . in another all but two could talk, relate, respond to praise.' In another statement one student teacher referred to pupils' level of attainment in key areas, in that 'Some children could read and write quite well, others with such great difficulty they had to be helped all the time.'

(6) How did the children respond to you?

The overwhelming impression felt by the student teachers was one of the friendliness of the children. 'They were open, friendly and responded well to my presence. A lot of the time particular pupils seemed to take great interest in me' and 'The children were very positive, immediately taking a liking to us and accepting me into their class' are comments which illustrate the warmth with which the student teachers were received. A few students were able to note that, with certain children, the desire to be close to them was more of an attention-seeking device which, when it proved to be unsuccessful, resulted in tantrums and physically aggressive behaviour, described as 'bouts of spitting, biting, scratching and pinching' or, more usually, as being 'clingy and wanting to hold your hand all the time.'

The behaviour of some children was obviously seen as markedly different from that of mainstream children. In at least one case this appeared to confirm a stereotypical view: 'The staff were sorting out a punching/strangling incident. Say no more.' One of the principal difficulties referred to by the student teachers was their inability to communicate with the children. This prompted one to suggest that 'you wouldn't get these types of children in an ordinary school'.

The student teachers did recognize a number of similarities between the behaviour of the children in the special schools and those they had encountered in mainstream schools. 'Some showed off, just like in mainstream schools' was one observation, whilst another noticed that 'It was good to see that these children could be just like other kids – naughty!'

Finally, some of the student teachers considered that the responses of the children may have been influenced by the fact that, in most of the schools, the staff were predominantly female: 'They loved having us there – again, particularly male in a very female-oriented environment'. One student teacher reported that 'It was suggested that I provided a role model for the boys which they did not have at the school as the majority of the staff were middle-aged women.' Leaving aside what might be construed as the perjorative nature of this comment, it is apparent that the student teachers were aware of the potential shortcoming of this aspect of the staffing profiles of many special schools.

Questions raised by the students' responses

The feedback provided by this group of student teachers can be considered firstly in terms of the success, or otherwise, of the two-day special school visits themselves and secondly as a means of ascertaining the value of building into a one-year course of teacher training a specific SEN component. An analysis of each of these may, in addition, provide a critique concerning current ITT arrangements for teachers. Each of these will now be considered so that, in summary, a suggestion can be outlined for future development in the training process of all student teachers which incorporates some experiences in special schools.

Eleven student teachers made unsolicited comments at the end of their questionnaires: each of these stated that, in the opinion of these students, the visits should be seen as an essential part of their one-year course of training. Amongst the comments illustrative of this were that the visits had been 'An enjoyable and valuable experience, especially for PE students' and that 'This was a useful, enjoyable and moving part of the course.' The importance of the visits to the student teachers was reinforced by the recommendation that it 'Would have been better placed at an earlier part of the course', a suggestion which was repeated verbally by the students during the visits. One even felt that 'The visit should have lasted much longer . . . say one week, or even two.' Taking these and the questionnaire responses into account the overall impression given by the student teachers appeared to be that some experience of the work of special schools should be an essential part of their training.

The student teachers' comments concerning their visits to special schools could also be used as a means of informally evaluating the generic SEN input during an ITT course. The analysis provided above suggests mixed results. The student teachers indicate that, in a number of important areas, the SEN course had been only partly successful. They tended to use descriptions of pupils which focused upon disability rather than learning difficulty; very few student teachers referred to the positive attributes of a pupil's learning behaviour (although frequent comment was forthcoming regarding the positive social attributes of the children); and, most importantly, several students were still inclined to use definitional terms which are, at best, old-fashioned but could, more importantly, be construed as being deficit oriented. Nevertheless, a number of student teachers had recognized that the SEN course which they had followed had provided some basis for understanding the work of a very specialized type of special school: 'Thank goodness we had a bit of prior information about what goes on in these schools – that made it less of a shock.'

The current approach to SEN in ITT courses has been briefly outlined in this chapter. The responses of the student teachers to their special school visits provide a means of emphasizing some of the problems inherent in existing training practice. They also, and rather worryingly, suggest that many new-comers to the teaching profession will be bringing with them an old-fashioned, deficit-laden view of special schools and what goes on in them. At the same time, however, the student teacher comments may also be used to validate a number of areas of potential development, and hence a source of optimism. In all honesty, though, the latter is not borne out by recent officially stated views on teacher education.

Thus the position of SEN in ITT courses still seems to be viewed as marginalized from the main activity of training student teachers in sets of competencies. In this respect it should be noted that the recently published surveys of new teachers in schools (OFSTED, 1993a) and of the training of primary teachers (OFSTED, 1993b) make no specific mention of SEN. The former focuses upon differentiation to address 'the challenge of meeting the needs of the range of abilities to be found in any one class' (p. 20). Prior to this, HMI, in its survey of school-based ITT, had also omitted an SEN overview (DES, 1991). Thus, whilst explicitly acknowledging that the integration of statemented children within mainstream schools is a fundamental policy initiative (DES, 1990b), there has been little evidence to support a view that the recommendations of Circular 3/84 have been reinforced in recent statements concerning the SEN content of ITT courses.

This tenuous situation has been summarized by Thomas, who states that

The success of higher education training institutions in providing appropriate preparation for pre-service teachers to meet special needs has been variable. They have found themselves . . . coping with this problem through either ghetto-izing special needs into strictly cabined timetable slots . . . or relying on a diffusion model in which the quality control over subject specialist tutors' input was at best partial, and at worse, non existent.

(Thomas, 1993, p. 113)

It may be argued that the student teachers, whose comments form the basis of this account, provide evidence that, in spite of their participation in a compulsory course in SEN, they still acknowledge important gaps in their initial experiences.

Further, it may be suggested that if the special school, and the children and staff within it, are not to remain 'a Cinderella dimension, attracting to it marginalized teachers as well as marginalized pupils' (Thomas, 1993) there ought to be a more dynamic interpretation of school-based work in ITT. In this the role of the special school itself should be seen as crucial, and visits to them should be regarded as a compulsory area of student teacher experience, rather than an 'unexpected bonus' (Hackney, 1990). This may provide an important initiative in enabling the work of special schools, their pupils, teachers and helpers, to be more effective as a central resource, rather than as 'sidings into which special needs problems disappear' (Dyson and Gains, 1993)

For the reader

Try to emulate the students described in this chapter. Visit, as and when you can, a different kind of school from your own. (You can often do this when half-term dates in neighbouring boroughs do not coincide, or by arranging an exchange with a friend.) People working in special schools will find it just as salutary to visit ordinary schools.

11

They Told Me He Would Be a Vegetable: Parents' Views

Sarah Sandow

On a recent in-service course, teachers were asked to write a brief account of an interview with the parent of a child with special educational needs. The following paragraph was written in response to this request, and was based on such an encounter.

> When X. was younger, my relationship with the professionals was based on fear. I really believed I could give them no useful information regarding X. I thought my views were irrelevant and very few of the professionals I met did anything to convince me otherwise. It seemed to me that my opinion was asked more out of politeness than for any other reason. As I had more contact with other parents through self-help groups, I began to realize my views were important and that I could affect the decisions made about my son. I spent a lot of energy asserting my rights and at this time I rejected most of the advice offered solely because it came from professionals and I decided they did not have my best interests at heart. It was only when X. was in his twenties that I actually felt I had some form of equality. I think it was because the times had changed and listening to parents was becoming more fashionable. Although I felt at this stage my views were listened to I never got over this feeling that I had created a problem and they were sorting it out for me.
>
> (Ruth Corben)[1]

These simple sentences almost make this chapter redundant because they encapsulate the way in which many parent–professional relationships have developed over the past quarter century. However, there are still some issues relating to the experiences and contributions of parents which should be explored. The past twenty-five years or so cover the period in which I have been personally concerned with the parents of children with special educational needs. Early encounters as a peripatetic home teacher attached to a special school alerted me to the experience of parents which corresponded fairly closely to that described in the paragraph quoted above.

Discovering the problem

One thing has not changed. Parents do not appear to have any more positive experiences in their first encounters with professionals than they did when Brock (1976, p. 149) wrote, 'We began to feel that many people were becoming fascinated by us as a problem and not attempting an answer. We were left alone to present our specimen for further analysis, or to use him as material for endless questionnaires whose conclusions, if any, we never saw.'

Twenty-three years later, McKay and Hersey (1990) found that 70 per cent of their sample of parents were dissatisfied with their early contacts with health professionals. The reasons included lack of explanation, many visits before the problem was recognized, and the manner of imparting information. Piper and Howlin (1992) showed that parents of children whose problems were not evident at birth were similarly critical of professional attitudes and practices. They took the view that healthcare professionals gave too little information, asked too many personal questions, asked for information which had already been given and kept people waiting unnecessarily. The picture is depressingly similar to that described by Brock. It may be argued that dissatisfaction is inevitable at such a stressful time. Shooting the messenger is an ancient therapy.

> Dr _____ told us she wouldn't live 48 hours and she'd be a cabbage, but she's proved him wrong, haven't you? In the beginning you want someone to blame. I knew before they told me, but when Dr _____ told me, I wanted to hit him. I told him he was a pig, he didn't care. I wanted to prove him wrong. He threw me out twice. Now I think he's marvellous. You get things in perspective, then you see how much they care.
>
> (Sandow, 1980)[2]

Cottrell and Summers (1989), discussing the communication of problematic diagnoses, noted that professionals needed to recognize that parents are observant and want an honest answer to their questions. The solution to this problem may be similar to that proposed by Hegarty in respect of partnership: it may not be possible to make it perfect, but a number of changes to procedure could improve matters. Piper and Howlin (1992)make sensible proposals: that parents should receive accurate information about the nature, location, length and personnel concerned with their child's assessment, should be given well-equipped waiting rooms including changing facilities, should have explained to them the nature and amount of any offered help and, perhaps most important, should receive a written summary of what was said and done, and be offered a follow-up appointment.

Parents' involvement in early education

In 1974 I began an action-research project, in which I attempted to engage parents of children with severe learning difficulties in individual programmes of teaching and learning with their children (Sandow *et al.*, 1981). Like many other early intervention programmes for young children with severe learning difficulties (SLD) devised during the 1970s, it was conceived within a framework of behavioural psychology, and the focus was intended to be on the progress made by the child during the two or three years between identification and the start of formal education. Preliminary assessments of the children were made (astonishingly it seems now) on the basis of preschool versions of standard IQ tests and behavioural assessments, and progress was similarly ascertained. Two groups of matched subjects were identified, and visits, during which a teaching programme was carried out, took place either at two-weekly or at eight-weekly intervals. All the parents were informed that the intention was to discover the optimum level of visiting. I expected that the children who received frequent visits would progress faster than the others, and for the first year this was indeed the case. However, to my astonishment, matters were reversed during the second year, when the infrequently visited group began to outstrip the others in progress. Although in the third year things began to even out, both groups progressed more than a third distal control group who received no intervention.

What were the lessons from this study? First, that while any intervention was better than nothing, it was not necessarily the case that the more intense the intervention, the better. I hypothesized that parents who were visited less frequently were more able to take charge of the intervention themselves. Using terms which were not yet fashionable, they were 'empowered' rather than 'deskilled'. Anecdotal evidence of the way the parents in the second group tackled the intervention supported this interpretation.

As in many other programmes conducted during the later 1970s and early 1980s, the parents involved were enthusiastic about their participation and about their children's progress. In retrospect, it now appears that some of the best and most enduring features were those which were not easily quantifiable.

What I get from you is confidence and acceptance of anything he does. I don't feel he's a monster with you. I'd have been mental if you hadn't shown me how to deal with him.

Where she has been and what people have seen her, it's done a lot for her. What physio did was to show me what I could do with toys and that. Like with you, really; you came and showed me what to do with your bag and that, and then it was up to me to do it when you weren't there. I got my ideas from you like. Like the other day, when I gave her some happy families cards and I just picked out four and gave them to her and she just put them on the right ones straight off, not like she used to do just flick them with her fingers. Mind you she still wants to do that but I say no, you do what I want to do then you can play with them how you want. I wanted him to see what she could do you see, because he don't believe what she can do and he was surprised. Physio should be like that really, you think it's going to be what they do but really it's what you do in between. They ought to tell you that.

(Sandow, 1980)

Behavioural programmes for preschool children began to proliferate, and were epitomized by the Portage Project, a highly structured programme which originated in the USA and was adopted in this country, notably at the University of Southampton (Smith Kushlick and Glossop, 1977). The organization of Portage meant that the short visits were entirely concentrated on specific tasks for the children and their achievement, and there were at first few concessions to more intangible gains. This and similar programmes were not without their critics. It was argued that simple behavioural programmes ignored the familial context of early intervention, and that in promoting the 'parent as teacher' they ignored the 'parent as parent' (Raven, 1981).

More recently, intervention programmes such as Portage have adhered less rigidly to a strict behavioural model and have recognized that an element of counselling is a vital ingredient (Le Poidevin and Cameron, 1985). In other words, they have taken account of the transactional relationship between the individual family and the environment, of which the intervening agent – teacher, psychologist or paraprofessional – is a part. Simple intervention implies that an 'injection' of 'treatment' at a particular time can redirect a child's whole future and it is now recognized that this is an inadequate approach. However, it may be that the need for a family focus is honoured still more in the breach than in the observance. Mahoney and O'Sullivan (1990) describe a range of early intervention programmes in six states in the USA after Public Law 99–457 had advocated a family focus for intervention. They examined the projects to see if the 'individualized family service plans' (IFSPs) mandated by the law were in operation: plans which contextualized the child's programme within the family and sought to avoid a clinical model.

They found that in nearly 1,000 programmes, relatively few providers determined service objectives on the basis of family needs. Those who used the IFSPs were more likely to teach parents how to be advocates, to help parents use community resources, to counsel parents, and to provide opportunities for families to meet others similarly placed: '[The] findings suggest that many providers who are working with families are interpreting the family focussed agenda as an incentive to integrate families into traditional clinical service models' (Mahoney and O'Sullivan, 1990, p. 174).

Flagg-Williams (1991) also notes the change to an 'empowerment' model in which the family's coping skills are enhanced by access to information and an effective social network. She notes that

> given the strain on most parents' time and other resources, professionals' suggestions sometimes only serve to exacerbate problems. For example, simply doling out activities for parents to do such as support groups or home training, may not always be appropriate. Sometimes a 'respite' program for parents that gives them a break away from some of the stressors may be more helpful . . . Also, professionals need to be careful not to stereotype or label families based upon a view that all of them will have certain stressors. . . . Families may inadvertently be placed into a pathological perspective by professionals if the focus is only on the myriad of stressors found in the literature.
>
> (Flagg-Williams, 1991, p. 242)

Looking at the effects of his own programmes with children with Down's syndrome, Cunningham (1986) argued that in spite of the popularity of such programmes, real evidence of their efficacy was lacking; indeed there were indications that the children involved did no better with respect to changes in learning and behaviour than those who had not participated in an intervention programme, nor did their families show more cohesion or less stress. There was only one difference, which again appeared to relate to 'empowerment', in that mothers whose children had been included were more likely to seek help from professionals, and more likely to re-enter full- or part-time employment.

Appleton and Minchom (1991) describe five varieties of parent–professional relationships in the context of child development centres: the expert model, 'in which professionals assess and treat a particular problem without necessarily making careful reference to parental wishes, views and feelings'; the transplant model, in which 'parents carry through a particular assessment or treatment programme according to directions given by a professional' (e.g. Portage); a consumer rights model, in which 'professionals would bow to parents' wishes for specific interventions for a child'; a social network/systems model in which 'parents, children and therapists are regarded as part of a network of informal and formal developmental and social support'. Finally, they too propose an empowerment model which incorporates features of both the consumer rights and the social network/systems model, and which they claim is built upon strengths rather than upon deficits.

A further interesting development is the extension of the reflective practitioner model current in teacher education to working with parents. Easen, Kendall and Shaw (1992) describe a way of working with parents which parallels this approach and includes a wide range of therapeutic methods. In fact, it may be that in attempting to analyse the process of intervention researchers have been trying too hard to apply models or templates to processes which are considerably more nebulous. Reflection by professionals and parents may uncover themes and ways of working which are useful and innovative.

Ways of involving parents in the early education of children with special needs has changed a great deal since the early days. They have benefited from a broader base than the simple foundation in behavioural psychology with which they began. However, as the evidence from Mahoney and O'Sullivan suggests, it may not always be easy to change professional attitudes. A great deal may depend on who is leading the intervention – psychologists (as often in the USA), other professionals, paraprofessionals or teachers. In this country with a limited tradition of nursery education (and what there is under constant threat), it seems unlikely that teachers will be protagonists. Given the clear findings of early studies, that early intervention is only successful if intensive, long lasting and subsequently reinforced, the involvement of teachers could be indicated. However, the role is still wider than that of a conventional teacher. Buchan, Clemerson and Davis (1988) identify a 'parent adviser' who, trained in counselling as well as behaviour management, is able to recognize and respond to individual parent needs. It may be that the creative, eclectic orientation of such an adviser is still too difficult to accommodate in an age of 'competences'.

Partnership
In 1984 I began a second major project, in which parents' views of the process of 'statementing' according to the Education Act 1981 were gathered and compared with those of the professionals who assessed the children (Sandow, Stafford and Stafford, 1987). Once again there were some unexpected as well as some predictable findings. Among the latter, it was clear that parents' priorities were for detailed knowledge of their own child and his or her progress, and not for the expertise of the powerful consulting professionals. Hence, they valued the teacher and the speech therapist above the paedia-

trician and the psychologist. What was less expected, especially in the mid-1980s, was an indifference to the concept of partnership and a considerable suspicion of integration. Partnership had been a particular concern of the Warnock Report, and had been presented as an article of faith by, for example, Mittler and Mittler (1982). Findings such as ours suggested that professionals paid only lip service to the concept, in a context where they were anxious about their own roles and powers, and that parents, while they sought professional support and advice, did not regard themselves as partners, nor seek to do so.

There have been a number of attempts to define partnership. Pugh (1989) has defined it as a working relationship, in which there is a shared sense of purpose, mutual respect and negotiation. Wolfendale (1989) also defines it in terms of respect for parental expertise, shared responsibility and shared decision-making. This is very different from the professionally directed model espoused by Mittler. All the attempts at defining and promoting partnership with parents derive from the premise that the old-fashioned distancing between parents and teachers was a bad thing for each of them as well as for children. Bastiani (1987) identifies four ideologies of home–school relations, which he illustrates by reference to particular examples. These are: compensation, communication, accountability and participation. The sequence is partly, though not totally, chronological. Bastiani points out that the ethos of compensatory education still permeates many staff rooms today, even though

> [t]he idea of social engineering, however well intentioned, now seems to embody a rather mechanistic view of social behaviour and its capacity for change. However to this reader, it seems reinforced rather than modified as suggested by Bastiani, by . . . the way in which home–school relations are made (rather than predetermined by global factors) through the interaction of teachers, parents and pupils.
>
> (Bastiani, 1987, p. 94)

It is certainly the case that, when several groups of teachers on in-service courses have been asked recently which of Bastiani's models applied in their (ordinary and special) schools, most identified compensation as the most pervasive one.

In 1993 Bastiani argues for the 'unscrambling' of the concept of partnership, and describes it as 'complex and elusive'.

> Everyone's in favour of home–school partnership – whatever it is! But because it's a buzzword, there also tends to be a conspiracy to avoid looking at it too critically in case it falls apart or disagreements break out. . . . Perhaps it is more helpful to see partnership as a process, a stage in a

process or something to work towards rather than something that is a fixed state or readily achievable.

(Bastiani, 1993, p. 113)

In the same volume Hegarty (1993) discusses partnership in special education with an equally critical eye, and questions whether it can survive as a concept (as opposed to a set of activities) at a time when education is presented as just another service industry, as in Bastiani's (1987) accountability model. Hegarty focuses on four areas where partnership in the practical sense can occur: communication between home and school, involving parents in the curriculum, contributing to assessment, offering personal support, and facilitating liaison with other agencies. Of course all of these can and do occur, even if the word partnership is never used.

The National Curriculum Council (NCC, 1989) has recognized the importance of 'continuous communication with parents and parent–teacher support' and seeks to promote family involvement in supporting teaching programmes for children with special needs.

All parents are individuals

Byrne and Cunningham (1985) pointed out the tendency for researchers in the 1960s and 1970s to assume a homogeneity in the families of children with special needs, based on psychological assumptions about the nature of their experiences.[3] They note that studies conducted within this framework tended to ignore differences such as socio-economic status, family size and the degree of disability. The defining attribute was simply the presence of the handicapped child in the household. In the 1980s the emphasis changed. Studies began to emphasize, not the pathological features of families with handicapped children, but rather the effectiveness of many such families in dealing with the resulting problems, which could include accessing services and dealing with professionals. Identifying the positive aspects of adaptation, it was proposed, could be more useful than concentrating on the assumed pathology of families.

Byrne and Cunningham's paper was written in the context of the new, ecological approach to the analysis of human relations proposed by Bronfenbrenner (1979). As Thomas (1992) has suggested, an ecological analogy seems at first sight rather far-fetched, but it does permit a very powerful interpretation and frees the researcher from the rigidities of a simple behavioural model. Briefly, Bronfenbrenner suggests that human experience can be described as multilayered. Each individual exists within a more or less concentric pattern of relationships and influences. These are described as the microsystem, comprising the activities, roles and relationships nearest to the individual, which itself is 'nested' within a mesosystem, which has an important but less direct influence. In turn the mesosystem is contained within the exosystem and finally the whole is contained within the macrosystem. An example might be a close interdependent relationship between two members of a family; this is the microsystem. The same family may contain a number of microsystems, and is itself within an exosystem comprising a network of relationships and roles which may include extended family members, friends, neighbours and significant others. It may of course be geographically constrained as well. Finally, this exosystem is enclosed by the macrosystem of beliefs, habits, expectations and rules, which structure the whole system.

Of course each person may be a member of more than one microsystem, at school and work as well as at home, and thus come within the influence of different ecosystems. We have only to think of the change in our personal ecosystem which occurs when we are admitted to hospital, and with the name on our irremovable wristband, we immediately become powerless children, unable to make decisions, semi-detached from our normal mesosystem, but occupying a particular place in a new and uncomfortable one. Children may be part of one microsystem at school and another at home; hence the very different picture which parents may have from that which teachers perceive. The difference is not due (as was formerly believed) to myopia on the part of the parents.

An ecosystemic approach, as Garner has suggested in Chapter 8, helps to contextualize behaviour problems and issues and prevents oversimplification. Thomas (1992) exemplifies this by reference to the antecedents and the context of difficult behaviour in school, rather than just the consequences, and points out that it is often easier for the teacher to alter the former rather than the latter.

One important aspect of both natural and human ecosystems is the maintenance of equilibrium, but this always involves changes, shifts and swings of emphasis. In the garden, thrushes control the snail population, which in turn protects the vegetation. An excess of magpies, predators on young thrushes, has the secondary effect of allowing an increase in the snail population which then requires control by other means. (I will not digress into an essay on snail control, but obviously some methods will themselves upset the ecological balance.) The human ecosystem also changes over time, sometimes slowly, between generations, sometimes quickly as a result of disaster, war or even change of government. So not only are all families different, they also change as micro- or mesosystems over time. These changes can and will occur at all levels within the system: in the microsystem relationships will change and develop, in the mesosystem whole households (and schools) will reorganize themselves and at the exosystemic level patterns of employment, housing or population distribution will alter. Finally the whole ethos which governs and structures the system as a whole is constantly changing. So parental priorities within a needs-based educational system are different from those within a system focused on achievement.[4] Further, the existence of high levels of unemployment among school-leavers will change the ecological map both for families with children who have learning difficulties and for those, less often heard, whose children are seen as presenting behavioural difficulties.

For those working with parents, all of this means that we must concentrate on identifying strategies rather than implementing tactics. The expert-oriented practice which we now find unacceptable may have been valid in the 1970s, and certainly it had some effect. But, like slug pellets, it may not be ecologically sound. Parents in the 1990s have learned to be less dependent, notwithstanding the political view that many are too dependent on the welfare state. They have become customers, and that in turn alters the role of the provider.

The attempts at defining partnership are a response to this fluidity, and it is not surprising that as Wolfendale (1989) has suggested, it is a slippery concept.

The forgotten parents

The literature about parental involvement in special education has included a substantial amount from parents themselves. Parents like Brock (1976) quoted above and Hannam (1975) were influential in shaping a new professional approach. However, most parents have written about children with learning difficulties. There appears to be little evidence that parents whose children are seen as disruptive have the ear of the professionals to the same extent. A careful literature search has revealed only one recent paper, in which Smith (1992b) argues that parents of seriously disturbed children are not well served by professionals. Writing in a social work journal she points out the lack of privacy experienced by such parents. 'We live in the knowledge that someone is always looking in.' She suggests that professional lack of sensitivity to this issue is one of the primary reasons that families become distrustful and withdrawn. Previous accounts of parental views in this area have been confined to the views of parents sampled in the context of care proceedings. Many of those reported by Thoburn (1980) reflect the deep suspicion, in particular of social workers, whom parents felt had 'conned' them about their intentions with respect to their children. Similarly, Packman (1986) reports suspicion and hostility from parents towards social workers: 'If you call people in to help, you expect them to help. But they've just taken full control.' Although relatively little research has been done into this group it has shown that parents and social workers often have very different ideas about the solutions to problems (Kahan, 1989).

Aymer *et al.* (1991) demonstrated how when behaviour problems arose in young people, social class, race and gender affected the career pathways through which they were directed. While the disruptive children of middle-class parents tread a path via the paediatrician to therapy or counselling, in which their parents are respected participants, working-class children are more likely to be dealt with by the education welfare service and the social worker. Parents in this situation, as Smith also avers, are seen as part of the problem, not part of the solution. 'The only parental involvement that I perceive as acceptable to many helping professionals involves the passive role of the family in allowing itself to be "fixed"' (Smith, 1992b).

The Elton Report (DES, 1989c) addressed itself in only a limited way to the involvement of parents. It commented on the need for an effective working partnership, and showed that the authors were aware of the increase in family stress in the past two decades. However, it cites sources which emphasize the negative aspects of family life, such as criminality, neglect and poor supervision (West, 1982) and the pathological, such as depression and anxiety (Galloway, 1982). It appears that as far as children with behavioural difficulties are concerned, parents are right to feel blamed. At the same time, Bennathan (1992) noted the increase in exclusions from school, the phenomenon of 'voluntary' withdrawal, the decline in support services, the poverty of home tuition, reduction of and even bans on residential placements (such as Peper Harow, closed in spring 1993) by local authorities. There are few support groups for parents of disruptive children, and one family support service (Contact-a-family) admits that setting up contacts is extremely difficult. Parents remain isolated, and largely voiceless. This is one population whose views are still not being heard.

Conclusion

In this chapter I have discussed the changes in parents' views and in special education and the move from a simple compensatory model through the various versions of partnership, to the current recognition of the value of an ecosystemic approach. The proliferation of programmes involving parents has been too great to discuss all of them, but the reader is invited to explore the following for further consideration: Cunningham, C.C. and Davis, H. (1985) *Working with Parents: Frameworks for Collaboration*, Open University Press, Milton Keynes; Sandow, S. (1990) The pre-school years: early intervention and prevention, in P. Evans, and V. Verma (eds.) *Special Education: Past, Present and Future*, Falmer, London; Wolfendale, S. (1989) *Parental Involvement: Developing Networks between Home, School and Community*, Cassell, London.

New issues will always remain to be explored. In the field of severe learning difficulties, parents' views on the curriculum, especially the impact of the National Curriculum in special schools, have been explored (Bertrand, 1992) to some extent, but there remains more to be done in this area. Secondly, the effect of an enterprise model of education on parents' expectations of children with special needs needs examining. Thirdly, the explanatory power of the ecosystemic approach is exciting, but what will be the effect on practice? Finally, as emotional and behavioural problems demand ever more attention, the empowerment of these parents too should be addressed.

Notes
(1) Ruth Corben is a teacher of children with special educational needs, currently in a school for children with emotional and behavioural difficulties.
(2) Corbett in Chapter 4 presents an alternative to such an account.
(3) These echo the assumptions about the homogeneity of the population of students with emotional and behavioural difficulties noted by Garner in Chapter 8.
(4) Note Hinchcliffe's comments on this in Chapter 9.

For the reader
Apart from the extra reading suggested above, consider Corben's account at the beginning of this chapter. Discuss with a parent the issues raised. In what way are things changing, if they are?

12

Whose Special Need?

Sarah Sandow

Throughout this book the various contributors have been celebrating differences, and at the same time relishing their own ability to contribute to the integration of individuals within society as children and above all as adults. So it may be believed that the job of the various professionals is to iron out the differences as best they can, and that the best way to achieve this is to treat children as though they are all the same. This is far from the case. In Chapter 3 Carol Aubrey points out that the emphasis on *where* a child is educated, rather than *how*, has distracted attention from what actually happens in the classroom. She notes that an understanding of how learning takes place, as a 'transformative rather than cumulative' process has been pushed to one side in favour of where it should take place. The psychology of teaching and learning, derided as 'barmy theory' by the penultimate Education Secretary, Kenneth Clarke, cannot be ignored if those with special needs are to realize their full potential (which does not mean to be like everyone else). Now that so little space is left in teacher education for such things, the educational psychologist can perhaps play a part in promoting them to teachers and participating in their realization. In this context, Aubrey's prediction that educational psychologists will shortly abandon the curriculum to return to testing is highly disturbing.

Viv Hinchcliffe in Chapter 9 also demonstrates how the application of knowledge about cognitive and developmental psychology can have a direct effect on the curriculum for those with severe learning difficulties and on their ability to have at least some power over their lives. It is interesting to note how this is in contrast to the strict behavioural techniques which would undoubtedly have been the focus of such a chapter written, say, ten years ago. The readiness of psychologists and sociologists to re-examine practice and theory continually is an enduring feature of both disciplines.

In Chapter 4 Jenny Corbett has taken a dispassionate view of the medical model, examining the reasons for its power and its unpopularity. She has shown how medical attitudes have changed and how far doctors have learned to encourage and facilitate the empowerment of their patients and, most importantly, of parents. To abandon the expert role in favour of a participative one is a major change in the face of centuries of traditional practice. However, there may be a little way to go before there are no more sad publications such as those noted in Chapter 11, which detail the failures in communication which still take place. Collaboration, co-operation and the sharing of information in a holistic framework are also characteristic of the therapies discussed in Chapter 5, 6 and 7. Each of these has grown up in the shadow of the medical model. The various forms of psychotherapy and counselling are increasingly popular; counselling courses have never been so heavily subscribed. However, to survive, counselling must find ways of evaluating its successes which are recognizable in an age of performance indicators, and yet retain some construct validity. The same is true of occupational therapy, straddling uncomfortably the gulf between art and science. Paramedical therapists may struggle to survive as distinct professions in the reduced circumstances of the 1990s.

Philip Garner's two contributions to this book each show the importance of simplicity and respect as components of an enquiry. Asking disaffected school students what they think about their education reveals some unexpected responses, which show that they are not, as some would believe, a separate species. Sampling the responses of young new teachers before their perceptions are blunted is also salutary. It is sometimes the case that in discussing special education, we are speaking to a converted minority in a 'Does he take Sugar' ghetto, but the reactions of the unconverted are a valuable counter to the 'warm fuzzy' which can become habitual.

All of these perspectives take place within the overall legal framework described in Chapter 2. Lawyers design such systems on behalf of politicians who have their own agenda. Currently this agenda appears to include the marginalization of special educational needs, in favour of a cult of excellence which in psychological and sociological terms is ill-considered and incoherent. I believe it to be based on a concept of citizenship which embraces conformity but disallows creativity, idiosyncrasy and individual differences to a degree which will stifle individual and community development.

There exists a view that the norm is attainable and desirable. Common sense tells us that neither of these is the case. Once a norm is attained, it ceases to be the norm, for in the act of achievement the individual has effectively moved the goal-posts for all those who follow behind. As to whether it is desirable, the celebration of individual differences is theoretically part of our culture. The Western ideology is substantially distinguished as one of individuality. Is the desire really for individuality for ourselves and conformity for everyone else? More than ever since 1988, our education system is predicated on a limited range of skills which are seen as practical, useful or instrumental. A teaching philosophy which celebrates the differences between us may be inimical to this.

There is a paradox contained in our feelings about special education and those who receive it. On the one hand, there is an apparent consensus about including children within the ordinary education system, because we value them as individuals and seek to adapt the school and the curriculum to support them. The old Warnock continuum, criticized by Aubrey in Chapter 3 for its superficiality, expressed this unstructured altruism. The Education Reform Act, as noted by David Anderson-Ford in Chapter 2, challenged directly the principles of the 1981 Act and virtually ignored special education. After 1988 the constant reorganization of the curriculum in the context of an enterprise model of education has led to the rejection of individual differences in the reification of normality. Now, if children with special needs are to be included, they must fulfil the criteria of normality, presented as competence in the basic subjects and conformity to behavioural requirements.

Currently there is confusion about what is expected of teachers. 'Delivering' the National Curriculum, yes, but this is not all. A whole range of skills, ideas, and concepts contained within such subjects as personal and social education, are seen as the teacher's responsibility but do not occupy a central position in the National Curriculum and are devalued in an instrumental view of education. Similarly, cultural and creative activity is devalued in favour of an information-based interpretation of knowledge. However, within the special-school curriculum, social and creative activities have traditionally been as important as the 'basic skills'. Currently, it appears that the only acceptable aspects of education are those which can be tested and which are perceived as employment related. It is hard to see how such a vital activity as the teaching of the significance of mental state words as described by Hinchcliffe in Chapter 9 can be contained within such a regime. Such activities are quite unthinkable in an integrated system.

Here the ideologies of many special-school curricula are in conflict with the National Curriculum, even though most schools attempt to follow it. To participate fully in the integrated situation, the child 'must get the basics right', but for what? If one can't 'get the basics', is one debarred from participation? We could compare literature with music. In some schools the child who cannot read is still excluded from the broader curriculum, in order to devote more time to those things at which he or she has already failed. The principle of disapplication endorses this. However, many children who have problems with the written word can speak two languages, and music is not inaccessible to the child who cannot read music or play an instrument.

The management of ordinary schools requires that children progress at an approximately even pace through the system. That is normal, meaning customary. As Skrtic (1991) suggests, this is naive pragmatism: 'A model of analysis and problem resolution that is premised on an unreflective acceptance of the assumptions that lie behind social practices.' It is assumed that school organization is rational, therefore deviation is irrational.

It is also assumed that ontology is consonant with chronology, that annual increments in development, knowledge and skill are not only equal irrespective of period of time but are also approximately equivalent for all individuals. Long before the National Curriculum, Baer (1970) described this as a system, not of child psychology, but of age psychology in which it is assumed that the infant belongs in the same textbook as the ten-year-old and is separated from him by ten stages of equal length. 'Ordering by age, it appears, is at the same time ordering on many other dimensions of behaviour: elaboration, precision, complexity, strength, amount, variety and internal organisation' (Baer, 1970). It therefore follows that school failure is assumed to be pathological.

Such assumptions prevent a 'productive confrontation with uncertainty' (Skrtic, 1991), for as Baer (1970) suggests, 'development is largely an age-irrelevant concept'. Special educators have long recognized the truth of this, which means that they are philosophically at odds with the mainstream system. They recognize that children can only be measured with elastic rulers.

Special educators, however, have their own assumptions. Perceiving the distrust and misunderstanding offered to special education by some in the mainstream, and resisting the drift back to categorization (epitomized by the very terms of the questions regarding statementing issued by the House of Commons Education Committee 1992),[2] they have sometimes promoted integration in circumstances where it cannot be justified, and where the benefits are questionable.

Sometimes in the 1980s it has seemed as though special educators were too anxious to smash the system. Special schools were rejected on the grounds that deviance is reinforced by them. Integration served as a rallying cry which united all those in special education who sought the inclusion of 'their' children within ordinary society. It was demanded regardless of the context, and regardless of whether the educational needs of the children were satisfied. This may be described as educational Maoism. Integration is still sometimes pursued irrespective of curriculum content; lack of communication and the failure to transfer skills from special educators can mean that only lip service is paid to individual differences by limited curriculum differentiation, often comprising merely a table in the corner with a special worksheet. The fervour of the proponents of the Regular Education Initiative (REI) in the USA is a case in point: Mostert (1991) argues persuasively that the assumptions of REI are founded on dogma rather than reality and actually prevent educational opportunities for children with special needs. Lieberman (1985) notes that 'in regular education, the system dictates the curriculum, in special education the child dictates the curriculum'.

But the school is not merely a place where teachers teach things to children. It is a social system (Woods, 1990) created by the participants, who are mainly children. It cannot be assumed that other children do not notice the different worksheet or the minimal response to the task, or the additional support given to the child with special needs. The concept of 'delivery' of the curriculum and the emphasis on assessment of the visible could mean that too little attention is paid to school processes other than the curriculum overtly offered. Superficially, the emphasis is on inclusion, defeating alienation, but the hidden curriculum, including both teacher actions, timetables, classroom geography and pupil attitudes, may be very different.

There are also external dangers. Practices devised for the best of intentions may be borrowed and extolled for quite other reasons. There is an analogy here with the concept of 'community care'. As in special education, the rhetoric of cost-effectiveness has been applied to the care of the elderly and of the mentally ill. Alongside ideas about 'value for money' there is an assumption that public services are almost by definition wasteful and inefficient (Trevillion, 1988–9). The emphasis is on resource management, rather than on the content of programmes. Trevillion notes the emphasis in the Wagner Report (1988) on the community as the 'opposite of the stigmatising and coercive inheritance of the poor law . . . at the heart of the report is a belief that attitudinal change and a set of rights guaranteed by a benevolent state will bring freedom and empowerment to those who are oppressed and powerless'. By contrast, the Griffiths Report (1988) 'seems to be identified with the "care market" as a transforming agency . . . it becomes "care management", a powerful business metaphor which attempts to banish the real world of pain, inequality and oppression to the margins of policy making' (Trevillion, 1988–9). Thus it seems that the benign, altruistic approaches epitomized by Wagner are transformed by Griffiths into something with very different objectives. Scull (1983) notes: 'all too often the "community" consists of the social wastelands that form the core of our cities, and "care" is another word for malign neglect'. Clearly, community care is cheap compared to asylum, and in a cost-effective model, probably the outcomes in terms of cure, employability, etc., are not dissimilar.

Further, the removal from the workforce of 'carers' is statistically advantageous.

Similarly, integration, as presently operationalized, is cheaper than special provision. It is notable in this context that the re-examination of the 1981 Act currently taking place is concerned entirely with the education of children with statements. The '18 per cent' (DES, 1978) have disappeared. In an era of high unemployment, educating those with special educational needs is not likely to be prioritized. There is consequently a press towards integration even if this is not the best educational solution, as there will, in any case, be little financial return arising from expenditure on special schools and off-site units. As in health, the cloak of respectability provided by the altruistic interpretation of integration, hides the financial motive. Just as there is already evidence that community care will degenerate for lack of proper funding as predicted by Hudson (1991), so special educators view with anxiety the disbanding of peripatetic special-needs support teams, the failure of LEAs to renew the appointment of special-needs advisers, and the disappearance of high-quality residential provision. In at least one borough known to the writer, the direct effect of the devolution of finance has been to remove the in-school special-needs support teachers and the borough-based special-needs advisory teachers at the same time as class sizes rose significantly.

Of course it would be as foolish to object to integration dogmatically as it would be to promote it for similar reasons. However, we must beware a situation where those with physical or sensory disabilities are included in ordinary schools mainly to provide a moral gymnasium for the able-bodied, while those with emotional or behavioural problems are banished, not for their own advantage but in order to prevent interference with the 'efficient education of others'. The rising exclusion rates suggest that this practice is increasing. Special schools generally offer precisely those qualities most valued by parents who are willing and able to pay for private education: small classes and individual attention. These were the main reasons given by 55 per cent of 78 parents who asked for special-school placements for their children in one LEA (Sandow, Stafford and Stafford, 1987). Such placements should always be available for those who need them, and as school and class numbers rise, they may be more needed than ever.

Conclusion
This book has asked the question, 'Whose special need?' The Warnock Committee replied that the special need was the child's, and the 1981 Act, flawed and restricted by lack of funds as it was, responded to this. During the 1980s the focus has gradually shifted, so that sometimes the special need seems

to be that of the State, or of the school, struggling to keep abreast of the competition by ridding itself of those who might lower the standards. Professionals, standing between the child and the state, and responding to the needs of children and parents, sometimes seem to have taken possession of the need themselves, for, uncomfortable as it is, the clientele helps to justify their existence. (I do not exclude myself from this statement.)

Having spent more than twenty years observing and working with a range of professionals and others in the service of children with special educational needs, I am struck more by the similarities than the differences between them. None of them is simply a deliverer of services, each recognizes the complexity and vibrancy of their subject.

There is, in 1993, as this volume has revealed, a considerable overlap in roles and ways of working. There is also a consensus about the need to empower parents and children. It is to be hoped that this will be accompanied by an increase in mutual understanding between professionals. It should at least be less likely in future that parents receive, as sometimes in the past, conflicting advice from various sources.

On the other hand, there is also considerable anxiety, as the professions struggle to retain their integrity at a time of constantly diminishing resources. It is vital that special skills and knowledge are not lost, in a general resource conglomerate, where a policy of 'best fit' replaces accurately focused provision. As has been emphasized in this final chapter, this also applies to school placement.

This book has been concerned to present a range of perspectives on a subject which is infinitely complex and endlessly fascinating. There is no teaching quite as satisfying as enabling the student with special educational needs to overcome the barriers to learning. While doing so the reader will develop her own perspective on special needs. Exploring and learning to understand the points of view represented here, and relating these reflectively to her own experience, that perspective may be enriched.

Notes

(1) The questions included the following: 'At what *level* of special educational need should children be statemented?' and 'At what *level* and extent of special need should primary and secondary schools be expected to make provision out of the resources under their control?' (my italics).

References

Adams, R. (1991) *Protests by Pupils: Empowerment, Schooling and the State*, Falmer, Basingstoke.

Appleton, P. and Minchom, P. E. (1991) Models of parent partnership and child development centres, *Child: Care, Health and Development*, Vol. 17, pp. 27–38.

Apter, S. (1982) *Troubled Children, Troubled Systems*, Pergamon, New York.

Arnot, M. and Barton, L. (eds.) (1992) *Voicing Concerns: Sociological Perspectives on Contemporary Education Reforms*, Triangle Books, Wallingford.

Ashman, A. and Conway, R. (1989) *Cognitive Strategies for Special Education*, Routledge, London.

Atkinson, D. and Williams, F. (1990) *Know Me as I Am: An Anthology of Prose, Poetry and Art by People with Learning Difficulties*, Hodder & Stoughton, London.

Aubrey, C. (1986a) Meeting the needs of severely handicapped children post-Warnock and the 1981 Education Act. Unpublished manuscript.

Aubrey, C. (1986b) Responses of school psychologists in two contrasting socio-cultural contexts to integration of handicapped pupils in the ordinary school, *School Psychology International*, Vol. 7, no. 1, pp. 27–34.

Aubrey, C. (1987) School psychology and special education in France with special reference to mental retardation, *Educational Psychology in Practice*, Vol. 3, no. 2, pp. 53–7.

Aubrey, C. (1988) Organisational school psychology and staff consultancy, in N. J. Jones and J. Sayer (eds.) *Management and the Psychology of Schooling*, The Falmer Press, Lewes.

Aubrey, C. (1990a) The development of the role of the school consultant as a means of dealing effectively with behaviour problems in schools, in R. M. Gupta (ed.) *Interventions with Children – Some Current Approaches*, Macmillan, London.

Aubrey, C. (1990b) *School Consultancy in the UK: Its Role and Contribution to Educational Change*, The Falmer Press, Lewes.

Aubrey, C. (1992) Educational psychology: the challenge for the 1990s, *Educational Psychology in Practice*, Vol. 7, no. 4, pp. 195–202.

Audit Commission and HMI (1992a) *Getting in on the Act*, HMSO, London.

Audit Commission and HMI (1992b) *Getting the Act Together*, HMSO, London.

Axline, V. (1947) *Play Therapy*, Churchill Livingstone, Edinburgh (reprinted by Longman, 1989).

Axline, V. (1964) *Dibs – In Search of Self*, Gollancz, London (reprinted by Penguin, 1990).

Aymer, C., Gittens, J., Hill, D., McLeod, I., Pitts, J., Rytovaata, M., Sturdevant, E., Wright, L. and Walker, M. (1991) The hardcore: taking young people out of secure institutions, in J. Dennington and J. Pitts (eds.) *Developing Services for Young People in Crisis*, Longman, Harlow.

Baer, D. (1970) An age irrelevant concept of development, *Merrill-Palmer Quarterly*, Vol. 16, pp. 238–45.

Ball, S. (1981) The sociology of education in developing countries, *British Journal of Sociology of Education*, Vol. 2, no. 3, pp. 301–13.

Barnes, C. (1992) *Disabling Imagery and the Media*, British Council of Organisations of Disabled People/Ryburn Publishing, Halifax.

Baron-Cohen, S., Leslie, A. and Frith, U. (1985) Does the autistic child have a 'theory of mind'? *Cognition*, Vol. 21, pp. 36–46.

Barris, R., Kielhofner, G. and Watts, J. H. (1983) *Psychosocial Occupational Therapy*, Ramsco Publishing Co., Laurel, Maryland.

Barton, L. and Oliver, M. (1992) Special needs: personal trouble or public issue? in M. Arnot and L. Barton (eds.) *Voicing Concerns: Sociological Perspectives on Contemporary Education Reforms*, Triangle Books, Wallingford.

Barton, L. and Tomlinson, S. (eds.) (1981) *Special Education: Policy, Practices and Social Issues*, Harper & Row, London.

Barton, L. and Tomlinson, S. (1984) *Special Education and Social Interests*, Croom Helm, London.

Bash, L., Coulby, D. and Jones, C. (1985) *Urban Schooling: Theory and Practice*, Holt, Rinehart & Winston, London.

Bastiani, J. (1987) *Perspectives on Home School Relations: Parents and Teachers*, Vol. 1, NFER-Nelson, Windsor.

Bastiani, J. (1993) Parents as partners – genuine progress or empty rhetoric, in P. Munn (ed.) *Parents and Schools: Customers, Managers or Partners*, Routledge, London, pp. 101–6.

Bates, E., Camaioni, L. and Volterra, V. (1975) The acquisition of performances prior to speech, *Merrill-Palmer Quarterly*, Vol. 21, pp. 205–26.

Bax, M. (1990) Young disabled adults: their needs, *Children and Society*, Vol. 4, no. 1, pp. 64–9.

BBCI (1992) *Advice Shop*, 15 November.

Bennathan, M. (1992) The care and education of troubled children, *Therapeutic Care and Education*, Vol. 1, pp. 37–49.

Berne, E. (1964) *Games People Play*, Penguin, Harmondsworth.

Bernstein, B. (1961) Social structure, language and learning, *Educational Research*, Vol. 3, pp. 163–76.

Bertrand, J. (1992) Severe learning difficulties, parents and the National Curriculum. Unpublished M. Ed. dissertation, Brunel University.

Bishop, D. V. M. (1979) Comprehension in developmental language disorders, *Developmental Medicine and Child Neurology*, Vol. 21, pp 225–38.

Bishop, D. V. M. (1982) Comprehension of spoken, written and signed sentences in childhood language disorders, *Journal of Child Psychiatry and Psychology*, Vol. 23, no. 1, pp. 1–20.

Blythe, B. L. G. (1985) Physiotherapy and mental handicap, *Physiotherapy*, Vol. 71, no. 3, pp. 115–18.

Bockoven, J. S. (1972) *Moral Treatment in Community Mental Health*, Springer, New York.

Booth, T. (1987) Labels and their consequences, in D. Lane and B. Stratford (eds.) *Current Approaches to Down's Syndrome*, Cassell, London.

Booth, T. (1992) Introduction to P. Russell, Affected by HIV and AIDS: cameos of children and young people, in T. Booth, W. Swann, M. Masterton and P. Potts (eds.) *Curriculum for Diversity in Education*, Routledge, London.

Bowles, S. and Gintis, H. (1976) *Schooling in Capitalist America*, Basic Books, New York.

BPS (British Psychological Society (1992) *The Feasibility of Developing National/Scottish Vocational Qualifications in Applied Psychology*, The British Psychological Society, Leicester.

Brock, M. (1976) The problem family, *Child: Care, Health and Development*, Vol. 2, pp. 39–43.

Bronfenbrenner, U. (1979) *The Ecology of Human Development*, Harvard University Press, Cambridge, Mass.

Brown, A. L. and Campione, J. C. (1986) Psychological theory and the study of learning disabilities, *American Psychologist*, Vol. 14, pp. 1059–68.

Buchan, L., Clemerson, J. and Davis, H. (1988) Working with families of children with special needs: the parent adviser scheme, *Child: Care, Health and Development*, Vol. 14, pp. 81–91.

Bullock, A. (1975) *A Language for Life* (Commission of Inquiry into Reading and the Use of English), HMSO, London.

Burnard, P. (1992) *Effective Communication Skills for Health Professionals*, Chapman & Hall, London.

Butler, R. A. (1971) *The Art of the Possible*, Hamish Hamilton, London.

Byrne, E. A. and Cunningham, C. C. (1985) The effects of mentally handicapped children on families: a conceptual review, *Journal of Child Psychology and Psychiatry*, Vol. 26, no. 6, pp. 847–64.

Camaioni, L. (1992) Mind knowledge in infancy; the emergence of intentional communication, *Early Development and Parenting*, Vol. 1, no. 1, pp. 15–22.

Campion, J. (1985) *The Child in Context*, Methuen, London.

Carrier, J. (1989) Sociological perspectives on special education, *New Education*, Vol. 11, no. 1, pp. 21–31.

Castle, E. (1958) *Moral Education in Christian Times*, Allen & Unwin, London.

Cattell, J. McK. (1890) Mental tests and measurements, *Mind*, Vol. 15, pp. 373–80.

Cazden, C. B. (1983) Play with language and metalinguistic awareness: one dimension of language experience, in Donaldson, M., Grieve, R. and Pratt, C. (eds.) *Early Childhood Development and Education* Blackwell, Oxford.

Center on Evaluation, Development and Research (1981) Practical application of research, *Phi Delta Kappan*, September, p. 5.

Chitty, C. (1989) *Towards a New Education System: The Victory of the New Right?* Falmer, Lewes.

Clements, J. (1987) *Severe Learning Disability and Psychological Handicap*, Wiley, New York.

Cogher, L., Savage, E. and Smith, M. (1992) *Cerebral Palsy: The Child and Young Person*, Chapman & Hall, London.

Conoley, J. C. and Conoley, C. W. (1982) *School Consultation: A Guide to Practice and Training*, Pergamon General Psychology, Oxford.

Corbett, J. A. (1981) Prevention of mental retardation, in B. Cooper (ed.) *Assessing the Handicaps and Needs of Mentally Retarded Children*, Academic Press, London.

Corbett, J. (1990) Watching and listening: a paediatrician's career, 1944–1986, *Disability, Handicap and Society*, Vol. 5, no. 2, pp. 185–98.

Corbett, J. and Barton, L. (1992) *A Struggle for Choice: Students with Special Needs in Transition to Adulthood*, Routledge, London.

Correia, S. (1993) Traditions and transitions: issues for the future, *British Journal of Occupational Therapy*, Vol. 56, no. 7, pp. 251–4.

COT (College of Occupational Therapists) (1989) *Occupational Therapy, An Emerging Profession in Health Care* (The Blom-Cooper Report), Duckworth, London.

Cottam, P. and Sutton, A. (1986) *Conductive Education*, Croom Helm, London.

Cottrell, D. J. and Summers, K. (1989) Communicating an evolutionary diagnosis of disability to parents, *Child: Care, Health and Development*, Vol. 16, no. 4, pp. 211–18.

Coupe, J., Barton, L., Barber, M., Collins, L., Levy, D. and Murphy, D. (1985)

The Affective Communication Assessment, Manchester Education Committee.

Coupe, J. and Goldbart, J. (1988) *Communication Before Speech*, Chapman & Hall, London.

Croll, P. and Moses, D. (1985) *One in Five: The Assessment and Incidence of Special Educational Needs*, Routledge & Kegan Paul, London.

Crompton, M. (1992) *Children and Counselling*, Edward Arnold, London.

CSLT (College of Speech and Language Therapists) (1991) *Communicating Quality: Professional Standards for Speech and Language Therapists*, CSLT, London.

Cunningham, C. C. (1986) The effect of early intervention on the occurrence and nature of behaviour problems in children with Down's syndrome. Summary of report to DHSS, Hester Adrian Research Centre, University of Manchester.

Da Costa, R. (1989) The parents' role in supporting children in education, in K. Mogford and J. Sadler (eds.) *Child Language Disability*, Multilingual Matters, Vol. 1, Clevedon.

Darwin, C. (1860) *On the Origin of Species by Natural Selection*, Murray, London.

David, R. and Smith, B. (1987) Preparing for collaborative working, *British Journal of Special Education*, Vol. 14, no. 1, pp. 19–23.

Delamothe, T. (1992) Poor Britain, *British Medical Journal*, Vol. 305, no. 6848, pp. 263–4.

DES (Ministry of Education) (1944) *Education Act*, HMSO, London.

DES (Department of Education and Science) (1970) *Education (Handicapped Children) Act*, HMSO, London.

DES (Department of Education and Science) (1972) *Speech Therapy Services*, (The Quirk Report), HMSO, London.

DES (Department of Education and Science) (1978) *The Education of Handicapped Children and Young People* (The Warnock Report), HMSO, London.

DES (Department of Education and Science) (1981) *Education Act*, HMSO, London.

DES (Department of Education and Science) (1988) *Education Reform Act: Local Management of Schools*, HMSO, London.

DES (Department of Education and Science) (1989a) *Assessment and Statements of Special Educational Need: Procedures within the Education, Health and Social Services*, Circular 22/89. HMSO, London.

DES (Department of Education and Science) (1989b) *National Curriculum: From Policy to Practice*, DES, London.

DES (Department of Education and Science) (1989c) *Discipline in Schools* (The Elton Report), HMSO, London.

DES (Department of Education and Science) (1990a) *Educational Psychology*

Services in England 1988–1989. A Report by HM Inspectorate, DES Publications, Stanmore.

DES (Department of Education and Science) (1990b) *Special Educational Needs in Initial Teacher Training,* DES, London.

DES (Department of Education and Science) (1991) *School-Based Initial Teacher Training in England and Wales,* HMSO, London.

DES (Department of Education and Science) (1992a) *The Children Act 1989,* Department of Health/HMSO, London.

DES (Department of Education and Science) (1992b) *Choice and Diversity* (White Paper), HMSO, London.

DfE (Department for Education) (1992) *Initial Teacher Training (Secondary Phase),* DfE, London.

DfE (Department for Education) (1993) *Education Act,* HMSO, London.

Douglas, J. (1964) *The Home and the School,* Panther, London.

Down, J. L. H. (1866) Some observations on an ethnic classification of idiots, in J. L. H. Down (1887) *On Some of the Mental Affections of Childhood and Youth,* Churchill, London.

Dryden, W. and Feltham, C. (1992) *Brief Counselling,* Open University Press, Milton Keynes.

Dyson, A. and Gains, C. (eds.) (1993) *Rethinking Special Needs in Mainstream Schools,* Fulton, London.

Easen, P., Kendall, P. and Shaw, J. (1992) Parents and educators: dialogue and development throught partnership, *Children and Society,* Vol. 6, no. 4, pp. 282–96.

Essen, J. and Wedge, P. (1982a) *Children in Adversity,* Heinemann Educational, London.

Essen, J. and Wedge, P. (1982b) *Continuities in Childhood Disadvantage,* Heinemann, London.

Eugenics Society (1934) *Report of the Departmental Committee on Sterilisation,* HMSO, London.

Everhart, R. (1983) *Reading, Writing and Resistance: Adolescence and Labor in a Junior High School,* Routledge & Kegan Paul, New York.

Fish, D. (1991) *Promoting Reflection,* West London Institute Press, Twickenham.

Flagg-Williams, J. (1991) Perspectives on working with parents of handicapped children, *Psychology in the Schools,* Vol. 28, pp. 238–46.

Flaskas, C. (1992) A reframe by any other name: on the process of reframing by strategic, Milan and analytic therapy, *Journal of Family Therapy,* Vol. 14, pp. 145–61.

Flavell, J. (1977) *Cognitive Development,* Prentice-Hall, Englewood Cliffs, New Jersey.

Flavell, J. (1981) Cognitive monitoring, in W. P. Dickson (ed.) *Children's Oral Communication Skills,* Academic Press, London.

Flavell, J., Speer, J. and Green, F. L. (1983) Development of the appearance –
reality distinction, *Cognitive Psychology*, Vol. 15, pp. 95–120.

Ford, J., Mongon, D. and Whelan, M. (1982) *Special Education and Social
Control: Invisible Disasters*, Routledge & Kegan Paul, London.

Fulcher, G. (1989) *Disabling Policies? A Comparative Approach to Education
Policy and Disability*, Falmer, Basingstoke.

Furlong, V. (1985) *The Deviant Pupil: Sociologial Perspectives*, Open University Press, Milton Keynes.

Furtwengler, W. (1990) Improving school discipline through student-teacher
involvement, in O. Moles (ed.) *Student Discipline Strategies*, State University
of New York.

Galloway, D. (1982) *Schools and Disruptive Pupils*, Longman, Harlow.

Garner, P. (1993) A comparative study of the views of the disruptive students in
England and the United States. Unpublished Ph. D. thesis, University of
London.

Glenn, S. M. (1987) Interactive approaches to working with children with
profound and multiple learning difficulties, in B. Smith (ed.) *Interactive
Approaches to the Education of Children with Severe Learning Difficulties*,
Westhill College, Birmingham.

Glenn, S. M. and Cunningham, C. C. (1984) The use of nursery rhymes in early
language learning with prelinguistic mentally handicapped children, *Exceptional Children*, Vol. 51, pp. 72–4.

Gold, K. (1991) Silver service, *Times Educational Supplement*, 7 June, pp. 25–6.

Goldbart, J. (1988) Communication for a purpose, in J. Coupe and J. Goldbart
(eds.) *Communication Before Speech*, Chapman & Hall, London.

Goodey, C. (1991) *Living in the Real World: Families Speak Out about Down's
Syndrome*, The Twenty-One Press, Newham Parents' Centre, London

Griffiths, R. (1988) *Community Care: Agenda for Action*, HMSO, London.

Gunzburg, H. C. (1966) *Progress Assessment Charts*, National Association for
Mental Health, London.

Hackney, A. (1990) Individual needs of student teachers, *Support for Learning*,
Vol. 5, no. 1, pp. 48–54.

Hannam, C. (1975) *Parents and Mentally Handicapped Children*, Penguin,
Harmondsworth.

Hannington, W. (1937) *The Problem of the Distressed Areas*, Victor Gollancz,
London.

Hearnshaw, L. S. (1979) *Cyril Burt, Psychologist*, Hodder & Stoughton,
London.

Hearst, D. (1992) Portrait revealed of a Russia that is killing itself, *Guardian*, 8
October, p. 20.

Hegarty, S. (1993) Home-school relations: a perspective from special education, in P. Munn (ed.) *Parents and Schools: Customers, Managers or
Partners?* Routledge, London.

Herbert, M. (1988) *Working with Children and their Families*, British Psychological Society in Association with Routledge, Leicester.

Herbert, M. (1993) *Working with Children and the Children Act: A Practical Guide for the Helping Professions*, British Psychological Society, Leicester.

Hewett, D. and Nind, M. (1992) Returning to the basics: a curriculum at Harperbury Hospital School, in T. Booth, W. Swann, M. Masterton and P. Potts (eds.) *Curricula for Diversity in Education*, Open University Press, Milton Keynes.

Hinchcliffe, V. and MSD1 course team (1992) Review of NCC Guidance 9, *Qwest*, no. 2, pp. 18–19.

Hinchcliffe, V. and Roberts, M. (1987) Developing social cognition and metacognition, in B. Smith (ed.) *Interactive Approaches to the Education of Children with Severe Learning Difficulties*, Westhill College, Birmingham.

Holinger, A. (1989) Parents' experiences of decision making about their children's special educational needs, in P. Widlake (ed.) *Special Children Handbook*, Hutchinson, London.

Hopkins, H. L. and Smith, H. D. (1971) *Willard and Spackman's Occupational Therapy*, Lippincott, Philadelphia.

Houghton, J., Bronicki, B. and Guess, D. (1987) Opportunities to express preferences and make choices among students with severe disabilities in classroom settings, *JASH*, Vol. 12, no. 1, pp. 18–27.

Howard, C. and Lloyd-Smith, M. (1990) Assessing the impact of legislation on special education policy – an historical analysis, *Journal of Education Policy*, no. 5, pp. 21–36.

Hudson, B. (1991) De-institutionalisation: what went wrong? *Disability, Handicap and Society*, Vol. 6, p. 1.

Hunt, P. (1985) *Clients' responses to marriage counselling*, Research Report No. 3, National Marriage Guidance Council, Rugby.

ILEA (Inner London Education Authority) (1986) *The Junior School Project: A Summary of the Main Report*, ILEA Research and Statistics Branch, London.

Jacobs, M. (1988) *Psychodynamic Counselling in Action*, Sage, London.

Johnston, R. and Magrab, P. (1976) *Developmental Disorders: Assessment, Treatment, Education*, University Park Press, Baltimore.

Jones, N. and Frederickson, N. (1990) *Refocusing Educational Psychology*, Falmer, London.

Jones, R. V. H. (1992) Getting better: education and the primary health care team, *British Medical Journal*, Vol. 305, no. 6852, pp. 506–8.

Judd, D. (1990) Psyche/soma issues for an adolescent with spina bifida and mental handicap, *Journal of Child Psychotherapy*, Vol. 16, no. 2, pp. 83–97.

Kahan, B. (1989) *Child Care Research Policy and Practice*, Hodder & Stoughton, London.

Kanner, L. (1944) Early infantile autism, *Journal of Paediatrics*, Vol. 25, pp. 211–17.

Kellmer-Pringle, M., Butler, N. and Davie, R. (1966) *Eleven Thousand Seven-Year-Olds: First Report of the National Development Study*, Longman, London.

Labov, W. (1969) The logic of non-standard English, *Language and Linguistics*, Vol. 22, pp. 1–31.

Laing, R. D. (1959) *The Divided Self*, Tavistock, London.

Lake, M. (1991) Surveying all the factors, *Language and Learning*, no. 6, pp. 8–23.

Lake, T. and Acheson, F. (1988) *Room to Listen, Room to Talk*, Bedford Square Press, London.

Lane, H. (1976) *The Wild Boy of Aveyron*, Allen & Unwin, London.

Leeming, K., Swann, W., Coupe, J. and Mittler, P. (1979) *Teaching Language and Communication to the Mentally Handicapped*, Evans/Methuen Educational, London.

Le Poidevin, S. and Cameron, J. (1985) Is there more to Portage than education? in B. Daly, J. Addington, S. Kerfoot and A. Sigston (eds.) *Portage: The Importance of Parents*, NFER-Nelson, Windsor.

Lieberman, L. M. (1985) Special education and regular education: a merger made in heaven? *Exceptional Children*, Vol. 51, no. 6, pp. 513–16.

Lunt, I. and Evans, J. (1991) *SENs Under LMS*, Institute of Education, London.

McGuire, B. E. and Tynan, M. E. (1992) Psychotherapy and counselling with people with moderate and severe intellectual disabilities, *Changes*, Vol. 10, no. 3, pp. 2,335–43.

McKay, M. and Hersey, O. (1990) From the other side: parents' views of their early contacts with health professionals, *Child: Care, Health and Development*, Vol. 16, no. 6, pp. 373–81.

McKelvey, J. and Kyriacou, C. (1985) Research on pupils as teacher evaluators, *Educational Studies*, Vol. 11, no. 1, pp. 27–31.

Macmillan, D. L., Keogh, B. K. and Jones, R. L. (1986) Special educational research on mildly handicapped learners, in M. C. Wittrock (ed.) *Handbook of Research on Teaching*, Macmillan, New York.

Mahoney, G. and O'Sullivan, P. (1990) Early intervention practices with families of children with handicaps, *Mental Retardation*, Vol. 28, no. 3, pp. 169–76.

Marsland, D. (1992) Methodological inadequacies in British social science, in S. Cang (ed.) *Festschrift for Elliott Jaques*, Cason Hall & Co., London.

Maseide, P. (1991) Possibly abusive, often benign, and always necessary. On power and domination in medical practice, *Sociology of Health and Illness*, Vol. 13, no. 4, pp. 545–61.

Mason, M. (1986) *Beyond the Label of Physical Disability: In our Own Right*, Community Services Volunteers, London.

Mason, M. (1992) Disabled parents, in R. Rieser and M. Mason (eds.) *Disability Equality in the Classroom: A Human Rights Issue*, Disability Equality in Education, London.

Masson, J. (1990) *Against Therapy*, Fontana, London.

Meadow, R. (ed.) (1991) *ABC of Child Abuse*, British Medical Journal Publications, London.

Meltzoff, A. N. and Moore, M. K. (1983) Newborn infants imitate adult facial gestures, *Child Development*, Vol. 54, pp. 702–9.

Merry, T. (1988) *A Guide to the Person-Centred Approach*, Association of Humanistic Psychology in Britain, London.

Meyer, A. (1922) The philosophy of occupational therapy, *Archives of Occupational Therapy*, Vol. 1, pp. 11–17.

Miller, G. A. (1973) *Psychology: The Science of Mental Life* (2nd edn), Harper & Row, New York.

Minuchin, S. and Fishman, H. C. (1981) *Family Therapy Techniques*, Harvard University Press, Cambridge, Mass.

Mitchels, B. (1991) Protecting the child, in R. Meadow (ed.) *ABC of Child Abuse*, British Medical Journal Publications, London.

Mittler, P. and Mittler, H. (1982) *Partnership with Parents: Developing Horizons in Special Education*, National Council for Special Education, Stratford.

Morel, B. A. (1857) *Traite de Degenerescences Physiques, Intellectuelles, et Morales de l' Espece Humaine*, Masson, Paris.

Morris, J. (1991) *Pride Against Prejudice: A Personal Politics of Disability*, The Women's Press, London.

Mortimore, P. and Blackstone, T. (1982) *Disadvantage and Education*, Heinemann, London.

Mostert, M. (1991) The Regular Education Initiative: strategy for denial of handicap and perpetuation of difference, *Disability, Handicap and Society*, Vol. 6, p. 2.

Muff, J. (1988) Of images and ideals: a look at socialization and sexism in nursing, in A. Hudson Jones (ed.) *Images of Nurses: Perspectives from History, Art and Literature*, University of Pennsylvania Press, Philadelphia.

Murphy, K. (1992) Parental perceptions of the professionals involved with children with special educational needs, in G. Vulliamy and R. Webb (eds.) *Teacher Research and Special Educational Needs*, David Fulton, London.

Murtaugh, M. and Zeitlin, A. (1989) How serious is the motivation problem in secondary special education? *The High School Journal*, LXIII, February/March.

NCC (National Curriculum Council) (1989) *Curriculum Guidance 2: A Curriculum for All*, NCC, York.

NCC (National Curriculum Council) (1992) *Curriculum Guidance 9: The National Curriculum and Pupils with Severe Learning Difficulties*, NCC, York.

NCC (National Curriculum Council) (1993) *Special Needs in the National Curriculum: Opportunity and Challenge*, NCC, York.

Netchine, S. and Netchine, G. (1976) Recherches recentes sur l'arrieration mentale, *Revue de Psychologie Appliquée*, Vol. 26, pp. 295–308.

Newsom, J. (1963) *Half Our Future* (The Newsom Report), HMSO, London.

Norwich, B. (1990) *Reappraising Special Needs Education*, Cassell, London.

OFSTED (Office for Standards in Education) (1993a) *The New Teacher in School*, HMSO, London.

OFSTED (Office for Standards in Education) (1993b) *The Training of Primary Teachers*, HMSO, London.

Oldfield, S. (1983) *The Counselling Relationship*, Routledge & Kegan Paul, London.

Oliver, M. (1989) Conductive education: if it wasn't so sad it would be funny, *Disability, Handicap and Society*, Vol. 4, no. 2, pp. 197–200.

Orton, C. (1989) The child with a medical problem in the ordinary school, in P. Widlake (ed.) *Special Children Handbook* Hutchinson, London.

Owen, I. R. (1992) What you say is what you do: a linguistic overview of counselling interventions, *Changes*, Vol. 10, no. 1, pp. 35–40.

Packman, J. (1986) *Who Needs Care?* Blackwell, Oxford.

Patterson, C. (1977) New approaches to counselling: healthy diversity or anti-therapeutic? *British Journal of Guidance and Counselling*, Vol. 5, no. 1, pp. 19–25.

Peat, M. (1981) Physiotherapy, art or science? *Physiotherapy Canada*, Vol. 33, no. 3, pp. 170–6.

Perner, J., Frith, U., Leslie, A. and Leekham, S. (1989) Exploration of the autistic child's theory of mind: knowledge, belief and communication, *Child Development*, vol. 60, 689–700.

Piper, E. and Howlin, P. (1992) Assessing and diagnosing developmental disorders that are not evident at birth: parental evaluations of intake procedures, *Child: Care, Health and Development*, Vol. 18, pp. 35–55.

Playfair, (1890) On primary and technical education, cited in Sellick (1968) *The New Education*, Pitman, London.

Popenoe, P. and Hill Johnson, R. (1920) *Applied Eugenics*, The Macmillan Company, New York.

Porter, J. (1992) What do pupils with severe learning difficulties understand about counting? *British Journal of Special Education*, Vol. 20, no. 2, pp. 72–5.

Potts, P. (1983) Medicine, morals and mental deficiency; the contribution of doctors to the development of special education in England, *Oxford Review of Education*, Vol. 9, no. 3, pp. 181–96.

Pugh, G. (1989) Parents and professionals in preschool services: is partnership possible? in S. Wolfendale (ed.) *Parental Involvement: Developing Networks between School, Home and Community*, Cassell, London.

Raven, A. (1981) Early intervention: a selective review of the literature, *CORE*, Vol. 5, no. 3, p. 81.

Reynolds, M. C. (1989) Students with special needs, in M. C. Reynolds (ed.) *Knowledge Base for the Beginning Teacher*, Pergamon, Oxford.

Rogers, C. (1983) *Freedom to Learn for the Eighties*, Charles Merrill, Columbus.

Russell, P. (1991) The Children Act: a challenge for all, *British Journal of Special Education*, Vol. 18, no. 3, pp. 115–18.

Russell, P. (1992) Affected by HIV and AIDS: cameos of children and young people, in T. Booth, W. Swann, M. Masterton and P. Potts (eds.) *Curricula for Diversity in Education*, Routledge, London.

Rutter, M. and Madge, N. (1976) *Cycles of Disadvantage*, Heinemann, London.

Rutter, M. Maughan, B., Mortimore, P., Ouston, J. and Smith, A. (1979) *Fifteen Thousand Hours* Open Books, London.

Sandow, S. (1980) Home intervention with the young handicapped child and his family. Unpublished Ph. D. thesis, University of Hull.

Sandow, S., Clarke, A. D. B., Cox, M. and Stewart, L. (1981) Home intervention with severely subnormal preschool children: a final report, *Child: Care, Health and Development*, Vol. 7, pp. 135–44.

Sandow, S., Stafford, D. and Stafford, P. (1987) *An Agreed Understanding? Parent Professional Communication and the 1981 Education Act*, NFER-Nelson, Windsor.

Schon, D. (1983) *The Reflective Practitioner*, Basic Books, New York.

Schostak, J. (1983) *Maladjusted Schooling*, The Falmer Press, Lewes.

Scull, A. (1983) Community corrections: panacea, progress or pretence? in D. Garland and P. Young (eds.) *The Power to Punish: Contemporary Penalty and Social Analysis*, Heinemann, London, Chapter 7, pp. 148–206.

Segal, J. (1989) Counselling people with disabilities /chronic illnesses, in W. Dryden, D. Charles-Edwards and R. Woolfe (eds.) *Handbook of Counselling in Britain*, Tavistock/Routledge, London, pp. 329–31.

Selleck, R. J. W. (1968) *The New Education*, Pitman, London.

Shilling, C. (1992) Reconceptualising structure and agency in the sociology of education: structuration theory and schooling, *British Journal of Sociology of Education*, Vol. 13, no. 1, pp. 69–87.

Shotter, J. (1980) Men the magicians: the duality of social beings and the structure of moral worlds, in A. J. Chapman and D. M. Jones (eds.) *Models of Man*, British Psychological Society, Leicester.

Simpson, J. and Smith, R. (1992) 'Macho' management in the NHS, *British Medical Journal*, Vol. 304, no. 6,842, p. 1,586.

Skrtic, T. M. (1991) The special education paradox: equity as the way to excellence, *Harvard Educational Review*, Vol. 61, no. 2, pp. 148–206.

Slagle, E. C. (1922) Training aides for mental patients, *Archives of Occupational Therapy*, Vol. 1, pp. 11–17.

Sloper, P. and Turner, S. (1992) Service needs of families of children with severe physical disability, *Child: Care, Health and Development*, Vol. 18, no. 5, pp. 259–82.

Smith, B. (1987) *Interactive Approaches to the Education of Children with Severe Learning Difficulties*, Westhill College, Birmingham.

Smith, B. (1991) *Interactive Approaches to Teaching the Core Subjects*, Lame Duck Publishing, Birmingham.

Smith, J. (1992) London's health care again, *British Medical Journal*, Vol 304, no. 6,843, pp. 1,646–7.

Smith, J. (1992) Parenting seriously disturbed children, *Social Work*, Vol. 37, no. 14, pp. 289–90.

Smith, J., Kushlick, A., and Glossop, C. (1977), *The Wessex Portage Project: a home teaching service for families with a preschool handicapped child*, Wessex Regional Health Authority Health Care Evaluation Research Team Report, 125, Winchester.

Solity, J. (1992) *Special Education*, Cassell, London.

Spearman, C. (1904) 'General intelligence' objectively determined and measured, *American Journal of Psychology*, Vol. 115, pp. 202–92.

Special Children (1993) Job losses begin to gather pace, *Special Children*, February, p. 5.

Staff of Rectory Paddock School (1983) *In Search of a Curriculum*, Robin Wren Publications, London.

Stallard, P. and Lenton, S. (1992) How satisfied are parents of pre-school children who have special needs with the services they have received? A consumer survey, *Child: Care, Health and Development*, Vol. 18, no. 4, pp. 197–205.

Stallworth, W., Frechtling, J. and Frankel, S. (1983) In-school suspension, a pilot programme, *ERS Spectrum*, Vol. 1, no. 1, pp. 23–31.

Stenhouse, L. (1979) Case study in comparative education: particularity and generalisation, *Comparative Education*, Vol. 15, no. 1, pp. 5–10.

Stern, D. (1977) *The First Relationship*, Harvard University Press, Cambridge, Mass.

Stevenson, D. (1991) Deviant students as a collective resource in classroom control, *Sociology of Education*, Vol. 64, pp. 127–33.

Stewart, J. and Pollack, G. (1991) A bereavement model for working with families of handicapped children, *Children and Society*, Vol. 5, no. 3, pp. 241–53.

Stokes, J. and Sinason, V. (1992) Secondary mental handicap as a defence, in A. Waitman and S. Conboy-Hill (eds.) *Psychotherapy and Mental Handicap*, Sage, London.

Sutcliffe, J. (1990) *Adults with Learning Difficulties: Education for Choice and*

Empowerment, National Institute of Adult Continuing Education/Open University Press, Leicester.

Sutcliffe, J. (1992) *Integration for Adults with Learning Difficulties*, National Institute of Adult Continuing Education, Leicester.

Sutton, A. (1981) The social role of educational psychology in the definition of educational subnormality, in L. Barton and S. Tomlinson (eds.) *Special Education: Policy and Social Issues*, Paul Chapman Publishing, London, pp. 109–32.

Sutton, A. (1992) Keeping specials 'special'. Unpublished paper delivered to the National Association of Head Teachers Conference, September, p. 2.

Sutton, C. (1989) The evaluation of counselling: a goal attainment approach, in W. Dryden (ed.) *Key Issues for Counselling in Action*, Sage, London.

Tharpe, R. G. and Gallimore, R. (1988) *Rousing Minds to Life*, Cambridge University Press.

Thoburn, J. (1980) *Captive Clients: Social Work with Families of Children Home on Trial*, Routledge & Kegan Paul, London.

Thomas, D. (1993) Gritty, sensible and utilitarian – the only model? Special educational needs, initial teacher training and professional development, in A. Dyson and C. Gains (eds.) *Rethinking Special Needs in Mainstream Schools*, Fulton, London.

Thomas, G. (1992) Ecological interventions, in S. Wolfendale, T. Bryans, M. Fox, A. Labram and A. Sigston (eds.) *The Profession and Practice of Educational Psychology*, Cassell, London.

Thorne, B. (1992) *Carl Rogers*, Sage, London.

Tizard, B., Carmichael, H., Hughes, M. and Pinkerton, G. (1980) Four-year olds talking to mothers and teachers, in L. A. Hersov and M. Berger (eds.) *Language and Language Disorders in Childhood*, Pergamon, Oxford.

Tomlinson, S. (1982) *A Sociology of Special Education*, Routledge & Kegan Paul, London.

Trevarthen, C. (1977) Descriptive analyses of infant communicative behaviour, in H. Schaffer (ed.) *Studies in Mother–Infant Interaction*, Academic Press, New York.

Trevillion, S. (1988–9) Griffiths and Wagner: which future for community care? *Critical Social Policy*, Vol. 8, no. 3, pp. 65–73.

Trower, P., Dasey, A. and Dryden, W. (1988) *Cognitive Behavioural Counselling in Action*, Sage, London.

Turner, B. S. (1987) *Medical Power and Social Knowledge*, Sage, London.

Urbano, M. T. (1992) *Preschool Children with Special Health Care Needs*, Chapman & Hall, London.

Vanes, A. (1992) Medicine and torture, *British Medical Journal*, Vol. 305, no. 8,650, pp. 380–1.

Wagner, G. (1988) *Residential Care: A Positive Choice*, National Institute for Social Work and HMSO, London.

Walrond-Skinner, S. (1976) *Family Therapy: The Treatment of Natural Systems*, Routledge & Kegan Paul, London.

Walton, G. (1990) Physiotherapy, in J. Hewlett (ed.) *Keyguide to Information Sources in Paramedical Sciences*, Mansell, London.

Ware, J. (1990) Can we and should we implement the National Curriulum for pupils with severe learning difficulties? in H. Daniels and J. Ware (eds.) *Special Educational Needs and the National Curriculum: The Impact of the Education Reform Act*, Kogan Page, London.

Warnock, M. (1991) Equality fifteen years on, *Oxford Review of Education*, Vol. 17, no. 2, pp. 145–53.

Warnock, M. (1992a) Special case in need of reform, *The Observer* (schools report), 18 October, p. 3 (delivered first to the National Association of Head Teachers Conference, September 1992).

Warnock, M. (1992b) Ethical challenges in embryo manipulation, *British Medical Journal*, Vol. 304, no. 6,833, pp. 1,045–9.

West, D. J. (1982) *Delinquency: Its Roots, Careers and Prospects*, Heinemann, London.

Williams, J. I. (1986) Physiotherapy is handling, *Physiotherapy*, Vol. 72, no. 2, pp. 66–70.

Willis, P. (1977) *Learning to Labour*, Saxon House, Farnborough.

Wilson, J. and Cowell, B. (1983) How shall we define handicap? *Special Education: Forward Trends*, Vol. 11, no. 2, pp. 33–5.

Winchurst, C., Kroese, B. and Adams, J. (1992) Assertiveness training for people with a mental handicap, *Mental Handicap*, Vol. 20, no. 3, pp. 97–101.

Wing, L. (1981) Language, social and cognitive impairments in autism and severe mental retardation, *Journal of Autism and Developmental Disorders*, Vol. 11, pp. 31–43.

Wiseman, M. R., Vizard, E., Bentovim, A. and Leventhal, J. (1992) Reliability of video taped interviews with children suspected of being sexually abused, *British Medical Journal*, Vol. 304, no. 6,834, pp. 1,089–91.

Wolfendale, S. (1989) Parental involvement and power-sharing in special needs, in S. Wolfendale (ed.) *Parental Involvement: Developing Networks between School, Home and Community*, Cassell, London.

Woods, P. (1979) *The Divided School*, Routledge & Kegan Paul, London.

Woods, P. (1990) *The Happiest Days?* Falmer, Basingstoke.

Woolman, J. (1758) The journal and essays, cited in Society of Friends (1960) *Christian Faith and Practice in the Experience of the Society of Friends*, Society of Friends, London.

Wright, J. A. (1992) Collaboration between teachers and speech therapists with language impaired children, in P. Fletcher and D. Hall (eds.) *Specific Speech and Language Disorders in Children*, Whurr Publishers Singular Publications, San Diego.

Yerxa, E. J. (1983) Audacious values: the energy source of occupational therapy practice, in G. Kielhofner (ed.) *Health through Occupation: Theory and Practice in Occupational Therapy*, F. A. Davis, Philadelphia.

Author Index

Vanes, A. 56
Volterra, V. 116

Walrond, Skinner, S. 69
Walton, G. 96
Ware, J. 119
Warnock, H.M. 20, 31–33, 35, 48
Watts, J.H. 92
Wedge, P. 8, 105
West, D. 110
Whelan, M. 107
Williams, F. 53
Williams, J.I. 97

Willis, P. 109
Wilson, J. 7
Winchurst, C. 116
Wing, L. 116
Wiseman, M. 55
Wolfendale, S. 147
Woods, P. 104, 109, 157
Woolman, J. 2

Yerxa, E.J. 92

Zeitlin, A. 112

Subject Index